BOOKKEEPING THE EASY WAY

SECOND EDITION

BOOKKEEPING THE EASY WAY

SECOND EDITION

WALLACE W. KRAVITZ

Formerly Business Education Chairman
Mineola High School
Mineola, New York

Barron's Educational Series, Inc.
New York / London / Toronto / Sydney

In this book the names of individuals and companies, and their type of business, are fictitious. Any similarity with the names and type of business of a real person or company is purely coincidental.

All inquiries should be addressed to:
Barron's Educational Series, Inc.
250 Wireless Boulevard
Hauppauge, New York 11788

Library of Congress Catalog Card No. 89-39382
International Standard Book No. 0-8120-4371-5

Library of Congress Cataloging in Publication Data
Kravitz, Wallace W.
Bookkeeping the easy way/Wallace W. Kravitz.—2nd ed.
p. cm.
ISBN 0-8120-4371-5
1. Bookkeeping. I. Title.
HF5635.K87 1990
657'.2—dc20 89-39382
CIP

PRINTED IN THE UNITED STATES OF AMERICA

0123 100 9876543

CONTENTS

CYCLE TWO A MERCHANDISING BUSINESS

PREFACE

Bookkeeping the Easy Way presents a simplified step-by-step approach to learning bookkeeping/accounting principles and practices. Understanding basic bookkeeping procedures is vital to developing an understanding of more advanced accounting theory and practice. Therefore, mastering the concepts of double-entry bookkeeping is a prerequisite to any further study.

This text is designed to be used in a variety of ways, depending on the need of the learner.

(1) Those who wish to study independently, at their own pace, will find this presentation clear and concise, without distractions.
(2) Those enrolled in adult education or continuing education courses will find that this text is designed for a relaxed, successful learning experience.
(3) Those who wish to study this subject in a one-semester course will find this work ideally arranged to coincide with most school half-year time schedules.
(4) Those who are having difficulty in grasping the fundamentals in a traditional introductory course in bookkeeping or accounting will find the text ideal for review or for remedial study.

Bookkeeping the Easy Way presents basic material for the individual, family, or sole proprietorship—a business owned by one person, typical of many business organizations. With improved bookkeeping skills, each individual, family, or business will gain a better command of available resources and help in planning a more profitable future.

Each chapter introduces one or two basic concepts of bookkeeping/accounting. Succeeding chapters build on the work that is covered in the preceding chapters. None can be omitted, nor should the order be changed. At the end of each chapter, students will find questions and problems, as well as analytical situations designed to explain not only the "how" but also—and equally important—the "why" of bookkeeping practices. These situations relate book learning to the business world. Including this work will result in a better understanding of legal obligations, a greater awareness of the private enterprise system, and, for learners, a career exploration experience.

A chapter on using a Combination Journal for personal or business records has been added to this revised edition. Many new answers to selected questions and problems have also been added to the final section of the book.

I would like to acknowledge the invaluable and inspirational aid of my wife, Mollie S. Kravitz, in helping with editorial work, as well as the typing of the original manuscript.

WALLACE W. KRAVITZ

CYCLE ONE
A Personal/Service-Type Business

WORDS TO REMEMBER
Assets all things of value that are *owned*
Liabilities all debts that are *owed*
Owner's Equity the value of one's *net worth, capital,* or *proprietorship*; the amount of assets remaining after all debts have been paid
Accounts Receivable amounts *due* from customers
Accounts Payable unpaid balances *owed* on debts

CHAPTER 1

ASSETS, LIABILITIES, AND OWNER'S EQUITY

The fundamental elements of all bookkeeping systems deal with keeping records for changes that occur in ASSETS, LIABILITIES, and OWNER'S EQUITY.

Definition of Assets

ASSETS are all things of value owned by an individual or business. Personal assets may include cash on hand, as well as savings and checking accounts, an automobile, and a home. Business assets may include similar items, as well as amounts due from customers—ACCOUNTS RECEIVABLE—and a building owned, not rented.

Examples of Assets—Personal and Business

A high school student's personal assets might include the following:

Cash on hand and in a savings account
Clothing
Sporting equipment
Jewelry
Bicycle

A family's personal assets might include the following:

Cash on hand, savings, and checking account
Home owned, not rented
Furniture and furnishings
Investments in stocks, bonds, and/or land

The assets of a small service-type business might include the following:

Cash on hand and in checking accounts
Building owned, not rented
Equipment
Supplies
Delivery truck

Consider the following list of assets used by the Evergreen Landscaping Service, a company owned by Thomas Morales, the proprietor:

Cash	$ 1,450
Truck	11,000
Haulaway Trailer	1,500
Customers' Accounts	3,600
Equipment	3,320
Office Furniture	750
Supplies	645
Total Assets	$22,265

Customers' accounts, the amounts due to be collected in a short time, are assets because they represent amounts that will be turned into cash as they are received. These are ACCOUNTS RECEIVABLE, and will be referred to by that term in this text.

Definition of Liabilities

LIABILITIES are the debts owed by an individual or business. Personal liabilities may include unpaid charge account balances, as well as amounts owed on a home and/or automobile loan. Business liabilities may include similar items: amounts owed, or ACCOUNTS PAYABLE.

Examples of Liabilities—Personal and Business

A high school student's personal liabilities might include the following:

Loan from parents to purchase car
Balance owed on school yearbook or class ring

A family's personal liabilities might include the following:

Balance owed on home mortgage
Balance owed on installment purchases
Unpaid household bills—gas, electric, telephone

Consider the following list of liabilities owed by the Evergreen Landscaping Service:

Truck Loan, Island National Bank	$6,200
Supplies Bought on Account	345
Equipment Bought on Account	1,000
Total Liabilities	$7,545

Definition of Owner's Equity

OWNER'S EQUITY is the net worth or capital of an individual or business. It is the amount of assets remaining after all liabilities are paid. To determine an individual's or family's owner's equity, total all assets, then deduct all liabilities. The difference is the owner's equity.

Examples of Owner's Equity

If a high school student's assets total $2,675, and liabilities total $450, the student's owner's equity equals $2,225:

Total Assets	$2,675
Less Total Liabilities	450
Owner's Equity, Net Worth, or Capital	$2,225

If a family's assets total $105,700, and liabilities total $44,960, the family's owner's equity equals $60,740:

Total Assets	$105,700
Less Total Liabilities	44,960
Owner's Equity, Net Worth, or Capital	$ 60,740

To determine Thomas Morales's owner's equity in the Evergreen Landscaping Service, follow the same calculation:

Total Assets	$22,265
Less Total Liabilities	7,545
Owner's Equity, Net Worth, or Capital	$14,720

Owner's equity is frequently referred to as NET WORTH, CAPITAL, or PROPRIETORSHIP. Individuals, however, usually refer to their owner's equity as "net worth" or "capital." A business might use all of these terms; however, this text will use most frequently OWNER'S EQUITY and CAPITAL.

The Fundamental Bookkeeping Equation

The relationship among the three elements of bookkeeping—assets, liabilities, and owner's equity—may be stated as follows:

(1) ASSETS equal	(2) LIABILITIES plus	(3) OWNER'S EQUITY

Consider these in the following way:

ASSETS (everything of value *owned*)	LIABILITIES (all debts *owed*) plus OWNER'S EQUITY

An example of these three elements as they apply to Thomas Morales's truck is:

Truck

Original cost	$11,000	Balance owed to bank	$ 6,200
		and	
		Morales's equity in truck	4,800
Total	$11,000	Total	$11,000

These three elements of bookkeeping may be stated as an equation:

$$\begin{array}{rcccl} \text{Assets} & = & \text{Liabilities} & + & \text{Owner's Equity} \\ \$11{,}000 & = & \$6{,}200 & + & \$4{,}800 \end{array}$$

or, simply,

$$A = L + OE$$

If owner's equity is referred to as capital, the equation is restated as

$$A = L + C$$

Variations of the Fundamental Equation

When any two of the fundamental elements are known, the third can be found. If assets total $10,000 and liabilities total $4,000, owner's equity equals $6,000. Assets minus liabilities equal owner's equity, or

$$A - L = OE$$

If assets total $12,835 and owner's equity totals $7,000, liabilities equal $5,835. It is also true that assets minus owner's equity equal liabilities, or

$$A - OE = L$$

If liabilities total $16,000 and owner's equity totals $22,900, assets equal $38,900. It is also true that liabilities plus owner's equity equal assets. This reverses the sides of the fundamental bookkeeping equation:

$$L + OE = A$$

These examples illustrate the variations of the fundamental bookkeeping/accounting equation: $A = L + OE$. All of these are true statements, whether for an individual, a family, or a business.

YOU SHOULD REMEMBER

All assets are subject to *two* claims—those to whom debts are owed, and those of the owner(s).

In listing claims against assets, claims of those to whom debts are owed *always* come before claims of the owner(s).

KNOW YOUR VOCABULARY

Use each of the following words or terms in a statement relating to bookkeeping/accounting:

- Accounts payable
- Accounts receivable
- Asset(s)
- Capital
- Liabilities
- Net worth
- Owner's equity
- Proprietorship

QUESTIONS

Classify each of the following items by writing *Asset, Liability*, or *Owner's Equity* in the column at the right:

	Item	Classification
Example:	Cash on hand	Asset
1.	Automobile	1.
2.	Balance owed on loan	2.
3.	Gerald Smith's capital	3.
4.	Supplies on hand	4.
5.	Personal clothes	5.
6.	Charge account balances	6.
7.	One's net worth	7.
8.	Bank loan	8.
9.	Allison Paris, account receivable	9.
10.	Panos & George, account payable	10.

PROBLEMS

1–1 Complete each of the fundamental bookkeeping equations so that each will be a true statement.

	Assets	= Liabilities	+ Owner's Equity
Example:	$ 10,500	$ 4,000	?($6,500)
1.	$ 15,750	$ 4,250	?
2.	24,900	?	$ 21,200
3.	?	5,000	12,500
4.	24,742.50	8,655.40	?
5.	31,070.92	?	22,501.85
6.	175,882.35	68,951.39	?
7.	?	58,042.78	152,775.56
8.	229,953.11	?	189,638.63
9.	686,020.49	114,362.74	?
10.	?	330,172.41	786,570.87

THINK IT OVER

Jack Calhoun's assets total $22,500; his liabilities total $7,500.

Mary Winslow's assets total $30,000; her owner's equity totals $25,000.

Which of these two individuals has a stronger "financial situation" or is better able to pay all debts owed? What other information might be needed in order to give a more definite answer?

WORDS TO REMEMBER

Account *each specific item* listed as either an asset, a liability, or an owner's equity

Business Transaction something that occurs, causing at least *two changes in accounts*

Investment a transaction made by an owner that *directly increases capital*, owner's equity

CHAPTER 2 BUSINESS TRANSACTIONS AND CHANGES IN THE FUNDAMENTAL BOOKKEEPING EQUATION

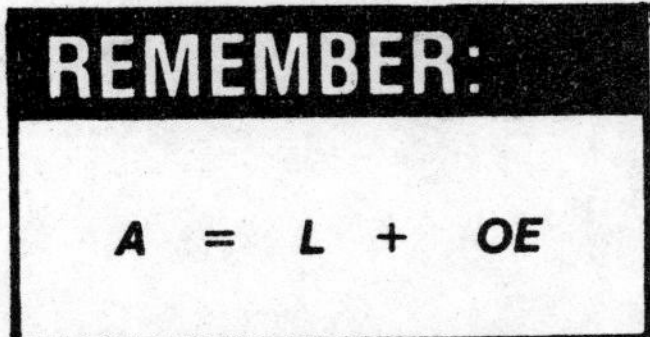

A BUSINESS TRANSACTION always results in at least two changes in the fundamental bookkeeping equation. Since both sides of this equation must be equal, a transaction that changes total assets must also change either total liabilities or total owner's equity.

Each item listed as either an asset, a liability, or an owner's equity is referred to as an ACCOUNT and is given a title—the Cash account, Truck account, Island National Bank account, Thomas Morales's Capital account, and so on.

Transactions Increasing Accounts

Assume that Morales, the owner of the Evergreen Landscaping Service, borrows $2,500 cash from the Island National Bank. The original bookkeeping equation showed:

Assets	=	Liabilities	+	Owner's Equity
$22,265	=	$7,545	+	$14,720

With the cash borrowed, the equation changes because the asset account, Cash, increases and the liability account, Island National Bank, increases:

Assets	=	Liabilities	+	Owner's Equity
$22,265		$ 7,545		$14,720
+ 2,500		+ 2,500		---
$24,765	=	$10,045	+	$14,720

Because this transaction resulted in two account increases, total assets increased and total liabilities increased.

Assume that Morales takes $5,000 of his personal cash to make an additional INVESTMENT in this business. The equation now shows an increase in the Cash account and an increase in Thomas Morales's Capital account:

Assets	=	Liabilities	+	Owner's Equity
$24,765		$10,045		$14,720
+ 5,000		---		+ 5,000
$29,765	=	$10,045	+	$19,720

Because this transaction also resulted in two account increases, total assets increased and total owner's equity increased.

Transactions Decreasing Accounts

Assume that Morales pays $1,000 cash to the Island National Bank as part payment on the truck loan. The equation now shows a decrease in the Cash account and a decrease in the Island National Bank account:

Assets	=	Liabilities	+	Owner's Equity
$29,765		$10,045		$19,720
− 1,000		− 1,000		---
$28,765	=	$ 9,045	+	$19,720

Because this transaction resulted in two account decreases, total assets decreased and total liabilities decreased.

Transactions That Increase and Decrease Accounts

Some transactions may change two accounts on the *same side* of the equation without changing any totals. Assume that Morales bought $100 worth of supplies, paying cash for them. His Cash account decreased by $100, while his Supplies account increased by $100, with no change in total assets.

All transactions cause two (or more, as will be shown later) changes in accounts. These changes may result in

(1) two increases,
(2) two decreases, or
(3) one increase and one decrease.

When transactions result in two account increases or two account decreases, totals on both sides of the fundamental equation change:

	A	=	L	+	OE	
(1)	$10,000		$2,000		$8,000	
	+ 1,500		+ 1,500		---	(two increases)
	$11,500	=	$3,500	+	$8,000	
(2)	− 500		− 500		---	(two decreases)
	$11,000	=	$3,000	+	$8,000	
(3)	+ 350					(one increase,
	$11,350					
	− 350					one decrease)
	$11,000	=	$3,000	+	$8,000	

YOU SHOULD REMEMBER

All transactions cause at least two changes in accounts. Either:
—two accounts increase, or
—two accounts decrease, or
—one account increases, as one account decreases.

KNOW YOUR VOCABULARY

Use each of the following words or terms in a statement relating to bookkeeping/accounting:

Account
Business transaction
Investment

QUESTIONS

Classify each of the following accounts as an asset, liability, or owner's equity. Indicate on which side of the fundamental equation—left or right—each account would appear.

	Account	Classification	Side
Example:	Cash (checking account)	Asset	Left
1.	Delivery truck	1.	
2.	Account payable, J. Glover	2.	
3.	Paul Jacob, Capital	3.	
4.	Account receivable, K. Day	4.	
5.	Balance due J. C. Woolco	5.	
6.	Customer's account balance	6.	
7.	Equipment	7.	
8.	Balance owed on truck	8.	
9.	Stamp collection	9.	
10.	Proprietor's claim	10.	

PROBLEMS

2–1 Write the words *Increase* or *Decrease*, or both words, or *None*, to show any change(s) in TOTAL assets, liabilities, and owner's equity for each of the following transactions:

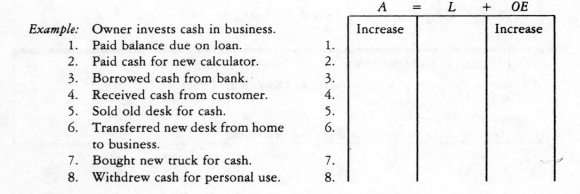

			A	= *L*	+ *OE*
Example:	Owner invests cash in business.		Increase		Increase
1.	Paid balance due on loan.	1.			
2.	Paid cash for new calculator.	2.			
3.	Borrowed cash from bank.	3.			
4.	Received cash from customer.	4.			
5.	Sold old desk for cash.	5.			
6.	Transferred new desk from home to business.	6.			
7.	Bought new truck for cash.	7.			
8.	Withdrew cash for personal use.	8.			

2–2 For each of the following business transactions, add or subtract the amounts to update total assets, liabilities, and owner's equity:

Example: Karen Glaser, owner, invested $15,000 in a dry-cleaning business.

1. Bought $2,000 worth of equipment, paying cash.
2. Borrowed $7,500 from River National Bank.
3. Bought $450 worth of supplies, paying cash.
4. Bought a truck for $12,000, paying cash.
5. Made a $1,500 payment on loan to River National Bank.

	A	= L	+ OE
Start with	$14,250	$4,250	$10,000
Example:	+ 15,000	---	+ 15,000
	$29,250	$4,250	$25,000
1.			
2.			
3.			
4.			
5.			

THINK IT OVER

Kenneth Lee operates a computer software business. He has a $16,000 cash balance. New equipment needed to develop the latest type of programs for his clients will cost $20,000. This will require some borrowing in order to pay for it. Lee wants to use $6,000 of cash from his business, arranging a bank loan for the balance.

What will be the amount of the loan? What changes will occur in the fundamental bookkeeping equation? Does Lee have any other choice in deciding how to buy this equipment?

WORDS TO REMEMBER

Account Form the arrangement of a *balance sheet*, with *assets* listed *on the left side*, *liabilities* and *owner's equity on the right side*

Balance Sheet a financial statement that lists all *assets owned* and all *claims against assets*, thus revealing one's *financial condition*

Creditor one to whom a debt is *owed*

Fiscal Period the *length of time* covered by the financial statements

THE BALANCE SHEET

REMEMBER:

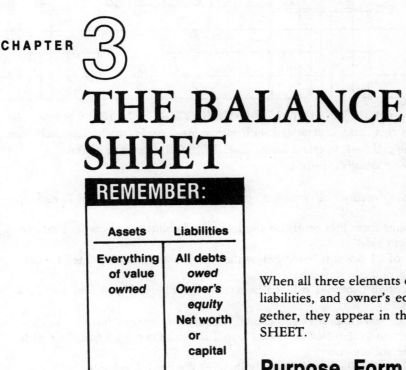

Assets	Liabilities
Everything of value owned	All debts owed Owner's equity Net worth or capital

When all three elements of bookkeeping—assets, liabilities, and owner's equity—are examined together, they appear in the form of a BALANCE SHEET.

Purpose, Form, and Content

A balance sheet is a financial statement or business form that lists, as of a certain date, all assets owned and all claims against these assets. These claims are held by CREDITORS, to whom money is owed, and the owners themselves, in the form of their owner's equity. When arranged in this way, it is easy to see that the fundamental bookkeeping equation again holds true:

$$A = L + OE$$

A bookkeeper or accounting clerk prepared a balance sheet for Thomas Morales's business on September 30, 199–.

Evergreen Landscaping Service
Balance Sheet
September 30, 199-

Assets		Liabilities	
Cash	7850 00	Gardners Supply Co.	345 00
Truck	11000 00	Equipment Mfg. Corp.	1000 00
Haulaway Trailer	1500 00	Island National Bank	7700 00
Accounts Receivable	3600 00	Total Liabilities	9045 00
Equipment	3320 00	Owner's Equity	
Office Furniture	750 00	Thomas Morales, Capital	19720 00
Supplies	745 00	Total Liabilities &	
Total Assets	28765 00	Owner's Equity	28765 00

This balance sheet shows the FINANCIAL CONDITION of Morales's business on the specified date. When this form is arranged with two sides—assets on the left, liabilities and owner's equity on the right—it is called an ACCOUNT FORM balance sheet.

Note the following details carefully:

(1) The heading consists of "answers" to the questions WHO, WHAT, and WHEN.
(2) The account form lists assets on the left side, liabilities and owner's equity on the right side.
(3) The sum of all assets is listed below the last one and identified as "Total Assets."
(4) The sum of all liabilities is listed below the last one and identified as "Total Liabilities."
(5) The sum of total liabilities and capital is listed on the *same line level* as the total assets and identified as "Total Liabilities and Owner's Equity" or with acceptable abbreviations.
(6) The final total dollar amounts on both sides are double ruled.
(7) The dollar symbol, comma, and decimal point are not used in any bookkeeping form or statement.

(Single ruled lines indicate an addition or subtraction. Double ruled lines indicate the end of the work.)

Fundamental Bookkeeping Equation

The fundamental bookkeeping equation is clearly seen on each balance sheet. The dollar value of total assets on the left side equals the dollar value of the creditors' claims (liabilities) plus capital (owner's equity) on the right side.

As shown earlier, each business transaction changes the dollar values of two items listed on the balance sheet. Therefore, a balance sheet showing a new financial condition, or picture, could be developed after each transaction. However, hundreds of transactions may occur daily, weekly, or monthly, making it impractical to do this so often. Usually financial statements are prepared at the end of a definite period of time—the FISCAL PERIOD. This can be monthly, quarterly, semimonthly, or annually. A 12-month fiscal period, however, need not coincide with the 12 calendar months of the year. A fiscal year could run from July 1 to the following June 30, or from April 1 to the following March 31.

Changes in Owner's Equity

Many of the transactions that occur during a fiscal period result in changes in owner's equity. These changes will eventually show up as increases or decreases in the owner's capital account. The exact amount of change can be determined by completing the fundamental bookkeeping equation. In completing the balance sheet for the Evergreen Landscaping Service, Morales's capital could have been calculated by subtracting total liabilities from total assets:

$$\$28{,}765 - \$9{,}045 = \$19{,}720 \quad \text{or} \quad A - L = OE$$

YOU SHOULD REMEMBER

Three items in a statement heading explain WHO, WHAT, and WHEN.
Assets *equal liabilities plus owner's equity*, or
Assets *minus liabilities equal owner's equity*.

KNOW YOUR VOCABULARY

Use each of the following words or terms in a statement relating to bookkeeping/accounting:

Account form	Creditor
Balance sheet	Financial condition
Claims against assets	Fiscal period

QUESTIONS

1. What three questions are answered in the heading of a balance sheet?
2. How many days are there in each month?
3. What is the last day of a quarterly fiscal period beginning on July 1? On January 1? On October 1?
4. What determines that a balance sheet is "in balance"?
5. How can owner's equity be found if total assets and total liabilities are known?
6. Write the following amounts in a ruled form, arranged for addition, and find the total: \$7,650; \$19,560; \$835; \$2,750; \$182.

PROBLEMS

3–1 Identify each of the following items by writing *Asset*, *Liability*, or *Owner's Equity* in the column at the right:

	Item	Classification
Example:	Cash on hand	Asset
1.	Automobile	1.
2.	Balance owed on time purchase	2.
3.	Cash in bank	3.
4.	Owner's claim against assets	4.
5.	Supplies for business use	5.
6.	Personal clothing	6.
7.	Unpaid balance on charge account	7.
8.	Creditor's claim against assets	8.
9.	Net worth	9.
10.	Money borrowed	10.

3–2 Name the section of a balance sheet—Assets, Liabilities, or Owner's Equity—in which each of the following items should be located:

			Balance Sheet	
			Left Side	Right Side
Example:	Machinery		Asset	
1.	Supplies	1.		
2.	Amounts owed to creditors	2.		
3.	Tools	3.		
4.	Bank loan	4.		
5.	Office equipment	5.		
6.	Checking account balance	6.		
7.	Amount due from customer	7.		
8.	Owner's financial claim	8.		
9.	Furniture	9.		
10.	Capital	10.		

3–3 On August 31 of the current year, the following assets and liabilities were listed by Maria Lopez, owner of Maria's Beauty Salon:

Assets:	Cash	$1,750
	Furniture and Fixtures	8,900
	Beauty Supplies	600
Liabilities:	Regal Laundry	275
	Marvelle Corp.	2,500

Prepare a balance sheet for Maria's Beauty Salon on the date indicated. Use the form in this chapter (page 16) for your model.

3–4 Paul Whitefeather, an accountant, has the following business assets and liabilities:

Assets:	**Cash**	**$ 750**
	Office Machines	**3,500**
	Furniture and Fixtures	**3,150**
	Office Supplies	**285**
Liabilities:	**Kearney Evans Co.**	**650**
	Cal's Stationery Co.	**175**

Prepare a balance sheet for Paul Whitefeather, dated September 30 of the current year.

3–5 The Dramatic Society of your local school has the following assets and liabilities on October 31 of the current year:

Assets:	Cash	$ 60.00
	Scenery	750.00
	Costumes	480.00
	Make-up Supplies	64.50
	Scripts	35.00
Liabilities:	E. Exter (seamstress)	75.00
	Field Lumber Co.	100.00
	Rex Drugstore	22.75

Prepare a balance sheet for the Dramatic Society on the date indicated. Indicate the owner's equity as Dramatic Society, Capital.

3–6 Lady Cake Bake Shoppe reports the following assets and liabilities on July 31 of the current year:

Assets:	Cash	$ 1,250.00
	Building	68,500.00
	Bakery Equipment	26,200.00
	Furniture and Fixtures	6,300.00
	Supplies	1,800.00
Liabilities:	Mortgage Loan Owed to Madison Bank	23,575.00
	Bakery Supplies Co.	350.00
	Baking Equipment Co.	5,000.00

Prepare a balance sheet for the Lady Cake Bake Shoppe on the date indicated. Gustave Mueller is the owner.

THINK IT OVER

Consider your own personal financial position. Prepare a list of all the assets you own. Place an estimated (or known) value on each. Do you owe any debts? What is your net worth or capital? Prepare your own balance sheet, complete with heading.

Do the same for your family as a whole. Ask other members of the family for estimated values to place on all assets owned and all debts owed, if you are not certain of the amounts.

WORDS TO REMEMBER

Account Form the arrangement of each item in a *ledger*; *debits* entered *on the left side* and *credits* entered *on the right side*

Balance the *value of an account* at any given time, as at the end of a fiscal period

Credit (cr.) entries *on the right side* of any account

Debit (dr.) entries *on the left side* of any account

Ledger *all accounts*, taken together *as a group*, for the same individual or business

Double-Entry Bookkeeping a method of bookkeeping in which, for every transaction, *the amounts debited must equal the amounts credited* (Debits = Credits)

T-Account an accountant's device, in the form of *a large "T,"* used *to analyze* debit and credit *entries* for each transaction

CHAPTER 4

THE LEDGER

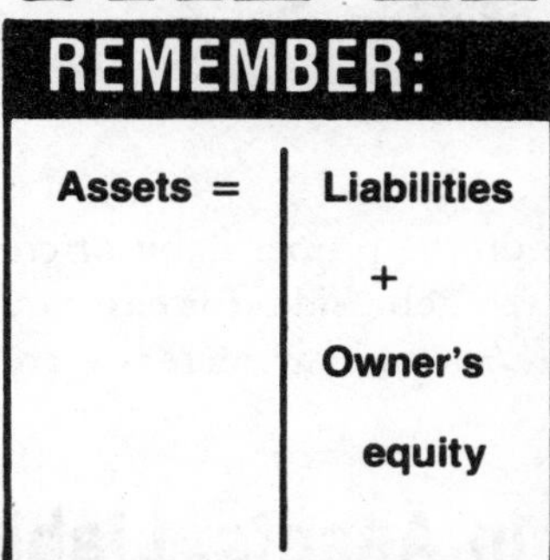

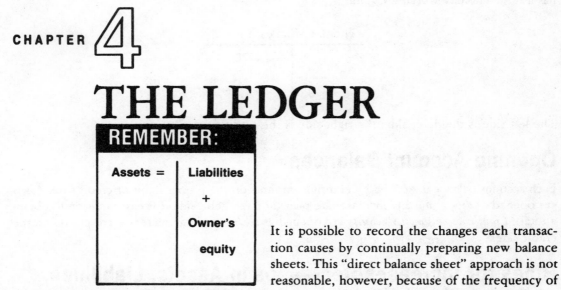

It is possible to record the changes each transaction causes by continually preparing new balance sheets. This "direct balance sheet" approach is not reasonable, however, because of the frequency of transactions and the amount of bookkeeping work involved. Furthermore, this does not provide a record that shows *how* each account changes; all that is shown is the final total in each account.

"T" Form of Accounts—Ruled Forms, Debit and Credit

To keep track of transactions and changes as they occur, a system of ACCOUNTS is used. The account form is used to record the changes that result in increases and decreases. Each item listed on a balance sheet is recorded in a separate account form. All accounts, taken together as one group, are called a LEDGER. The ruling for an account originates from the account form of a balance sheet: assets listed on the left side, liabilities and owner's equity on the right side.

Examine the Evergreen Landscaping Service's cash account, starting with an opening BALANCE of $1,450. (See page 4.) This account has a title: Cash. The left side of an account is the DEBIT side; the right side of an account is the CREDIT side.

Cash	
1450	

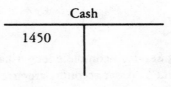

Each of the *assets* listed on page 4 would appear in the same way—as *debit balances*. Notice that they are in the form of an enlarged "T" and therefore are called T-ACCOUNTS.

Examine the T-account for Evergreen Landscaping Service's liability owed to Island National Bank. (See page 5.) This account has a title: Island National Bank. The left side is the debit side; the right side is the credit side.

Island National Bank	
	6200

Each of the *liabilities* listed on page 5 would appear in the same way—as a *credit balance.*

Examine Morales's owner's equity account: Thomas Morales, Capital. The account has a title: Thomas Morales, Capital.

Thomas Morales, Capital	
	14720

The left side is the debit side; the right side is the credit side.

Opening Account Balances

Each account balance is opened by entering amounts on the proper debit or credit side. *Assets* are opened as *debits*, and any increases are placed on the debit side (for easy addition to obtain a total). *Liabilities* and *owner's equity* are opened as *credits*, and any increases are placed on the credit side.

Rules for Increases/Decreases in Assets, Liabilities, and Owner's Equity

The accepted bookkeeping/accounting abbreviations for debit and credit are Dr. and Cr., or dr. and cr. These are used in various business forms. Written statements will, however, use the complete words. Note carefully the following statements:

(1) *Assets* are accounts that appear on the left-hand side of a balance sheet and will show *increases* by *debits*.
(2) *Liabilities* are accounts that appear on the right-hand side of a balance sheet and will show *increases* by *credits*.
(3) *Owner's equity* (*capital*) appears on the right-hand side of a balance sheet and will show *increases* by *credits*.

Assets	
Dr.	Cr.
+	

Liabilities	
Dr.	Cr.
	+

Owner's Equity	
Dr.	Cr.
	+

Evergreen Landscaping Service's complete ledger has been opened from the account information listed on pages 4 and 5. Asset accounts are arranged first, followed by liabilities and owner's equity accounts.

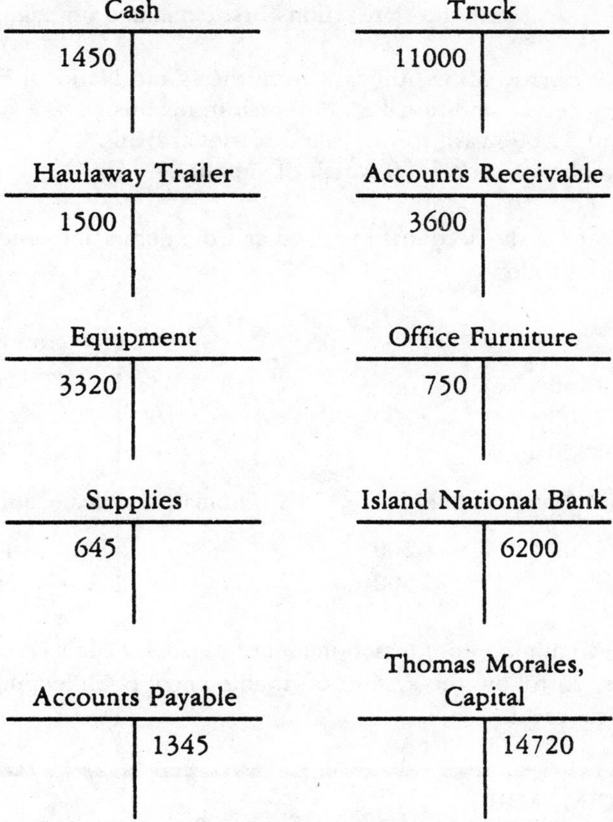

Each account receivable could have been listed in a separate T-account to show the individual amount *due from each customer*. In the same way, each account payable could have been listed in a separate T-account to show the individual amount *owed to each creditor*. One creditor was listed in a separate account—Island National Bank. It could have been combined with the other accounts payable for one total amount owed—$7,545.

Because assets increase by debits, it follows that any *asset decreases* are recorded as *credits*. Because liabilities and owner's equity increase by credits, it follows that any *liability* and *owner's equity decreases* are recorded as *debits*. The three T-accounts shown on page 24 can now be completed to illustrate the RULES OF DEBITS AND CREDITS:

(1) Assets increase by debits and decrease by credits.
(2) Liabilities increase by credits and decrease by debits.
(3) Owner's equity increases by a credit and decreases by a debit.

Assets		Liabilities		Owner's Equity	
Dr.	Cr.	Dr.	Cr.	Dr.	Cr.
+	−	−	+	−	+

Proving the Equality of Debits and Credits

As transactions occur, changes are recorded in accounts. For every transaction, at least one account will be debited and one will be credited. Even though each transaction changes two or more account balances, the fundamental bookkeeping/accounting equation will always be in balance: $A = L + OE$. This is the explanation of the theory of DOUBLE-ENTRY BOOKKEEPING: for every transaction debits always equal credits.

Reexamine in T-accounts the transactions first explained on pages 10 and 11:

(1) Morales borrowed $2,500 cash from the Island National Bank.
(2) He invested an additional $5,000 cash in his business.
(3) He paid $1,000 cash to the Island National Bank.
(4) He bought for cash $100 worth of supplies.

A *partial* ledger for the accounts involved and the debits and credits for (1), (2), (3), and (4) above is shown as follows:

Cash

	1450	(3)	1000
(1)	2500	(4)	100
(2)	5000		

Supplies

	645		
(4)	100		

Island National Bank

(3)	1000		6200
		(1)	2500

Thomas Morales, Capital

			14720
		(2)	5000

Notice that each numbered transaction identifies a debit and a credit of equal amount. This is helpful in order to follow the system of double-entry bookkeeping. For every transaction, debits must equal credits.

YOU SHOULD REMEMBER
In every transaction debits equal credits.
Assets increase by debits and decrease by credits.
Liabilities increase by credits and decrease by debits.
Owner's equity increases by credits and decreases by debits.

KNOW YOUR VOCABULARY

Use each of the following words or terms in a statement relating to bookkeeping/accounting:

Account form	Double-entry bookkeeping
Balance	Ledger
Credit (cr.)	Rules of debits and credits
Debit (dr.)	T-account

QUESTIONS

1. Which of the following statements is true?
   a) For *every* transaction, the account(s) debited equal the account(s) credited.
   b) For *every* transaction, the account(s) increased equal the account(s) decreased.
2. Explain why the incorrect statement in Question 1 is not true.
3. What would be the normal balance of any asset account?
4. On which side—debit or credit—do accounts decrease?

PROBLEMS

4–1 Emilee Suzanne listed the following account balances:

Cash	$1,245
Equipment	3,670
Supplies	430
Accounts Payable:	
L. D. Brown	400
J. C. Tucker	175

(1) Open a ledger of T-accounts for each of these accounts, including one for each creditor.

(2) Open a T-account to record Emilee Suzanne's capital, net worth, or owner's equity. Remember: $A - L = OE$.

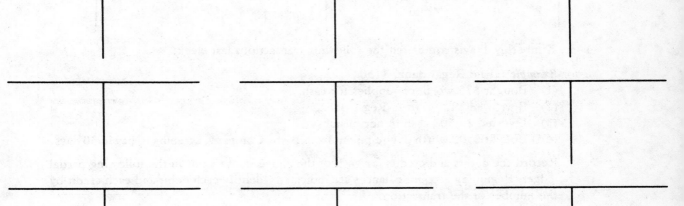

4–2 Paul Jacobs listed the following account balances:

Cash on Hand and in Bank	$1,305
Accounts Receivable:	
D. R. Able	150
M. O. Jackson	225
V. L. Witten	85
Truck	5,750
Supplies	395
Accounts Payable:	
City Trust Company	1,250
H. & H. Manufacturing Co.	800

(1) Open a ledger of T-accounts for each account, including Jacobs's owner's equity.

(2) Prove that Assets = Liabilities + Owner's Equity.

4–3 Kimberley Travis completed the following transactions last week:

Example: Paid Regal Bank, $150.
(1) Bought $75 worth of supplies for cash.
(2) Borrowed $1,000 from Regal Bank.
(3) Invested $2,500 cash in her business.
(4) Bought $500 worth of equipment from Bixby Company, agreeing to pay in 30 days.

Record the debits and credits for each of the above transactions in the following partial ledger. Beginning account balances are indicated. Identify each debit and each credit by the number of the transaction.

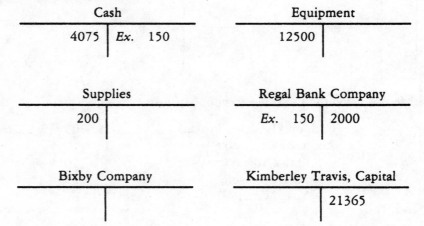

Cash	
4075	*Ex.* 150

Equipment	
12500	

Supplies	
200	

Regal Bank Company	
Ex. 150	2000

Bixby Company	

Kimberley Travis, Capital	
	21365

4–4 Using the transactions in Problem 4–3, indicate any increases or decreases in *total* assets, liabilities, and owner's equity.

Trans. No.	Assets	Liabilities	Owner's Equity
Example	Decrease	Decrease	
(1)			
(2)			
(3)			
(4)			

4–5 (1) Open T-accounts for Lori Luing, the owner of Luing's Answering Service, for the following balances, including her owner's equity:

Cash	$ 437.50
Accounts Receivable:	
H. L. Rhodes, MD	50.00
Mary Turner, MD	50.00
T. W. Vine, DDS	35.00
Equipment	2,650.00
Supplies	25.00
Accounts Payable:	
State Telephone Co.	215.00
Ace Electricians	65.00
Lori Luing, Capital	________ ?

(2) Complete each of the following transactions, indicating by letter the debits and credits:

a) Received $50, the amount due, from H. L. Rhodes, MD.
b) Paid $65, the amount owed, to Ace Electricians.
c) Bought $75 worth of supplies, paying cash.
d) Invested $500 cash in the business.
e) Received $25 on account from Mary Turner, MD.

(3) Prove that Assets = Liabilities + Owner's Equity.

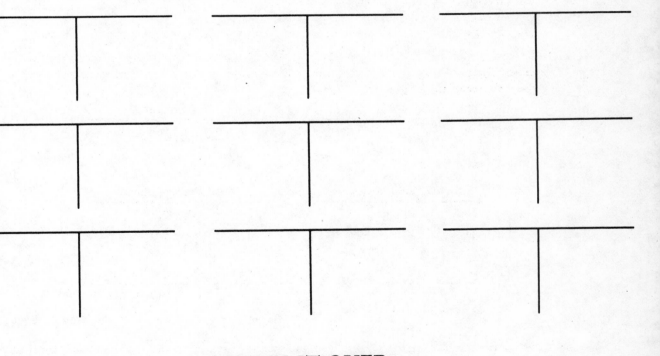

THINK IT OVER

Select any service-type business and consider the many different kinds of transactions that are carried on in any typical day. Think about the reason(s) why the owner is in business. What is his/her goal? What is the "profit motive" that keeps the owner going?

WORDS TO REMEMBER

Drawing Account the owner's special account for recording any *withdrawals for personal use*
Expenses *payments made* in connection with earning income or operating one's business
Net Income amount by which revenue exceeds expenses, *when income earned is greater than expenses*; a *profit*
Net Loss amount by which expenses exceed revenue, *when expenses are greater than income earned*
Revenue money or money equivalent earned during the fiscal period.

OWNER'S EQUITY ACCOUNTS

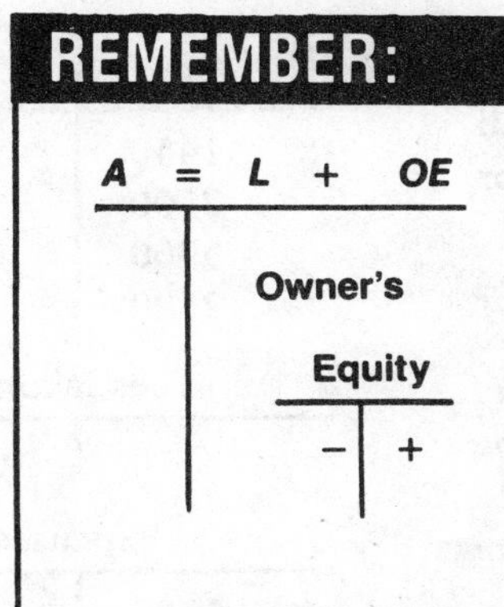

Revenue Accounts for Income Earned

A business earns its income (or REVENUE) by selling merchandise and/or services. In this section of this text, all revenue will be earned by charging fees for services performed by the business. The Evergreen Landscaping Service charges each customer a fee for the work performed on a regular basis—weekly or monthly. Special jobs, such as tree removals, are also a source of revenue. The term "revenue" will refer to various fees that are earned by services rendered to the customers of a business. In each case they will be identified by the account title, including the word "income."

Expenses

Any payments made in connection with the earning of revenue are called EXPENSES. These include such items as advertising, rent, employees' salaries, and utilities (heat, light, telephone).

Net Income/Net Loss

If, during a fiscal period, the revenue earned exceeds the total expenses, the business will have a PROFIT or NET INCOME:

$$\text{Revenue} > \text{Total Expenses} = \text{Net Income}$$

If, however, expenses exceed revenue, a NET LOSS will result:

Expenses > Revenue = Net Loss

(In these equations the symbol ">" means "is greater than.")

Effect of Revenue/Expenses on Owner's Equity

Whenever *revenue* is received, owner's equity is *increased*. Whenever *expenses* are paid, owner's equity is *decreased*. At the end of a fiscal period, if all revenue exceeds all expenses, the resulting net income belongs to the owner. Owner's equity will, therefore, be increased by that amount. If expenses exceed revenue, the resulting net loss is suffered by the owner. Owner's equity will, therefore, be decreased by that amount.

Assume that the Evergreen Landscaping Service earned $2,500 in fees last month, and expenses totaled $1,500 for the same period:

Revenue: Fees Income	$2,500
Expenses	1,500
Net Income	$1,000

Revenue and expense transactions will change account balances. The accounts listed on page 26 will change as follows: for the revenue earned (*a*), and for the expenses paid (*b*).

Additional accounts will be opened to record the revenue and expenses rather than recording these transactions directly in the owner's equity account. Because *revenue* increases owner's equity, it will be recorded as a *credit*. Because *expenses* decrease owner's equity, they will be recorded as a *debit*. (Expenses are combined in one T-account for this example.)

Cash

Debit	Credit
1450	1000
2500	100
5000	(*b*) 1500
(*a*) 2500	

Fees income

Debit	Credit
	(*a*) 2500

Expenses

Debit	Credit
(*b*) 1500	

By the end of the fiscal period, the fundamental bookkeeping/accounting equation will have changed:

All Assets,	29765	Liabilities,		9045
		Owner's Equity,	19720	
		+ Net Income	1000	20720
Total Assets	29765	= Total Liab. + OE		29765

Owner's Drawing Account

At any time the owner of a business may withdraw cash for personal use, very much like a salary. WITHDRAWALS by the owner, however, are not included with other expenses. Instead, a separate account is opened for the DRAWING ACCOUNT.

Effect of Withdrawal on Owner's Equity

Any *withdrawal* by the owner *decreases owner's equity*; therefore it must be recorded as a *debit*. Note the transaction to record Morales's withdrawal of $500 cash: transaction (*c*).

This transaction changes the fundamental bookkeeping equation: $500 less cash (assets) and $500 less capital (owner's equity).

Assets,	29765	Liab.,		9045	
–	500	OE,	20720		
		–	500	20220	
A	29265	= L	+ OE	29265	

Cash

Dr.	Cr.
1450	1000
2500	100
5000	1500
2500	(*c*) 500

Thomas Morales, Drawing

Dr.	Cr.
(*c*) 500	

Revenue and expenses are temporary owner's equity accounts. They change—increase and decrease—owner's equity. Compare a capital account with revenue and expense accounts:

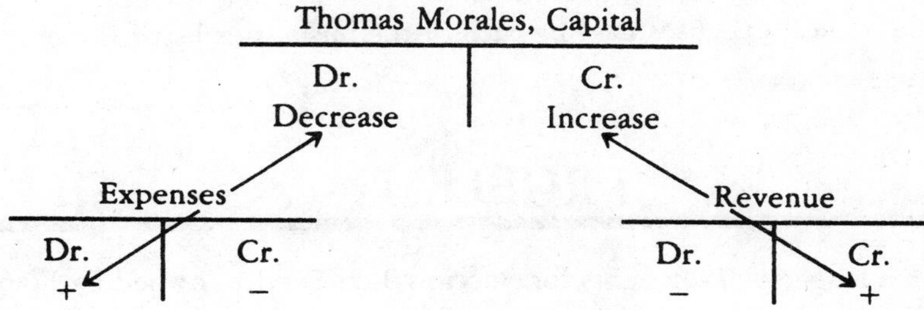

As *expenses increase* by *debits*, owner's equity decreases.
As *revenue increases* by *credits*, owner's equity increases.

When the owner has made a withdrawal during the fiscal period as well as earned a net income, owner's equity is determined as follows:

Owner's Equity		
Ruth Brown, Capital, October 1,		12 000
Net Income	800	
Less Withdrawals	650	
Net Increase in capital		150
Ruth Brown, Capital, October 31,		12 150

YOU SHOULD REMEMBER

Income *increases owner's equity*; therefore, *income accounts increase by credits.*
Expenses *decrease owner's equity*; therefore, *expense accounts increase by debits.*

KNOW YOUR VOCABULARY

Use each of the following words or terms in a statement relating to bookkeeping/accounting:

Drawing account	Profit
Expenses	Revenue
Net income	Withdrawals
Net loss	

QUESTIONS

1. What are the sources of revenue received by each of the following service businesses?
   a) A tailor
   b) A beauty salon
   c) An architect
   d) A lawyer
   e) A dentist
   f) An accountant
2. What are the typical expenses paid by each of the businesses listed in Question 1?

PROBLEMS

5–1 (1) Open a ledger of T-accounts for Puccio's Taxi Service, owned by Frank Puccio:

Assets:	Cash	$ 562
	Taxis (2)	28,000
	Supplies	150
Liabilities:	Landia National Bank	6,400
	Wilson Garage	75
OE:	Frank Puccio, Capital	?

Open T-accounts for each of these accounts, as well:
Frank Puccio, Drawing
Fare Income
Gas and Oil Expense
Repairs Expense
Salary Expense

(2) Record the following transactions, indicating by letter each of the debits and credits:
a) Collected $250 in fares.
b) Paid Landia National Bank, $100.
c) Paid driver's salary, $200.
d) Withdrew cash for personal use, $300.
e) Collected $325 in fares.
f) Paid for gasoline, $45.
g) Paid Wilson Garage, $75.
h) Paid for taxi repairs, $40.

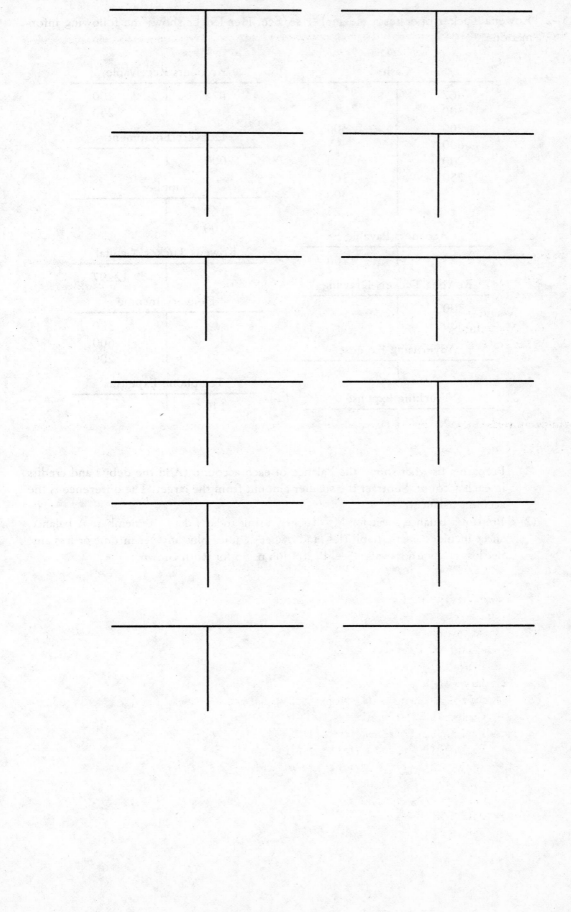

5–2 Rowena Tucker operates a messenger service. Her ledger shows the following information:

Cash	
462	75
300	75
200	300
600	95
200	140
250	100
	300
	25

Accounts Payable	
25	1100

Rowena Tucker, Drawing	
300	
300	

Advertising Expense	
95	

Trucking Expense	
75	
75	

Accounts Receivable	
875	200
	250

Delivery Equipment	
12000	

Supplies	
60	
100	

Rowena Tucker, Capital	
	12297

Delivery Income	
	300
	600
	200

Telephone Expense	
140	

(1) Prepare a list that shows the balance of each account. (Add the debits and credits in each account. Subtract the smaller amount from the larger. The difference is the account balance.)

(2) Prepare a balance sheet for Ms. Tucker, using today's date. Remember: A balance sheet includes assets, liabilities, and owner's equity plus any net income or less any net loss and withdrawals. (See illustration p. 33 for Ruth Brown.)

(1)

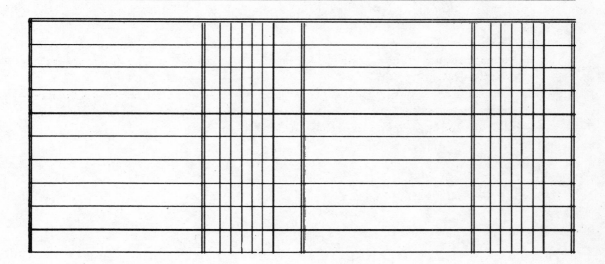

(2)

THINK IT OVER

James Lightfoot owns three sporting goods stores, each located in a suburban center near a large midwestern city. For several years he has had a net income. Last year, however, he had a small net loss. He is anxious to find the reason for this loss. Lightfoot maintains one ledger for his business. What would you recommend that he do differently, and why?

WORDS TO REMEMBER

Compound Entry a *journal* entry that consists of *one or more debits* that equal *one or more credits*
Journal *a book of original entry* recording transactions in *chronological order*
Simple Entry an entry that consists of *only one debit* that equals *one credit*
Voucher a *source document* that is the *evidence of a transaction*

TWO-COLUMN GENERAL JOURNAL

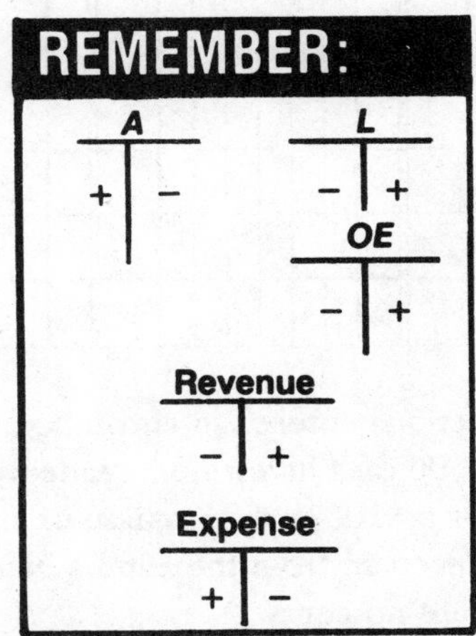

Records of business transactions can be entered directly into ledger accounts. However, DIRECT LEDGER bookkeeping can be a difficult and complicated procedure. Since each transaction involves at least one debit equal to one credit, examining one account gives only one half of the information about a transaction. If amounts are similar, finding the other half, even when numbered or lettered, may require a great deal of time. In order to tie together the debits and the credits of the same transaction, every account would have to be examined to find the matching amount.

Bookkeeping/accounting should be orderly. The direct ledger system does not give an orderly running record of all transactions day by day. If an error is made in recording—entering two debits or two credits instead of one of each, or reversing the accounts to be debited and credited, or changing the amount of a debit or credit—locating that error can become a very difficult, time-consuming process. Because there may be hundreds or more entries in a single day, week, or month, the bookkeeping clerk will have to examine each account to find the offsetting amounts in tracing an entry.

Book of Original Entry

To solve this problem, a system of JOURNALS can be used. A journal is a book of ORIGINAL ENTRY, where complete information about a transaction is first recorded. Each page is numbered; columns provide space for a complete date—year, month, day; names of accounts debited and credited; posting references (to be discussed in Chapter 7); and amount columns for debits and for credits. All entries are recorded in CHRONOLOGICAL order as they occur. All information—the date of the transaction, the accounts involved, the amount of each debit and each credit—and any needed explanation are included in this book, a general journal. It becomes the diary of the business for which it is kept.

JOURNAL Page 12

Date		Account Title	PR	Debit	Credit
199- Sept.	4	Cash		1500 00	
		George Corbo, Capital			1500 00
		Investment			
	7	Supplies		100 00	
		Cash			100 00
		Check No. 418			
	10	Cash		2000 00	
		Landia National Bank			2000 00
		30-day Loan, Note No. 25			

This general journal illustrates several transactions entered in chronological order on page 12. The first one, dated September 4, is for a $1,500 cash investment made by the owner, George Corbo. The second, dated September 7, is for a $100 cash purchase of supplies. The third, dated September 10, is for a $2,000 cash loan received from the Landia National Bank. Note that zeros are used, rather than a dash, to indicate no cents.

Source Documents

As transactions occur, SOURCE DOCUMENTS are prepared as evidence of these transactions. In some cases the source document may be referred to in the short explanation. A source document is any prepared form or VOUCHER, such as a check or check stub, a numbered bill for services, or a memorandum of a transaction. These will be discussed in more detail in Chapters 14, 15, and 16.

The bookkeeping clerk records additional entries on the next page of the journal, starting again with a complete date:

JOURNAL Page 13

Date		Account Title	PR	Debit	Credit
199- Sept.	15	Cash		50 00	
		Accounts Receivable (John Smith)		100 00	
		Fees Income			150 00
		Sales Slip No. 284			
	20	Equipment		800 00	
		Regional Supply Company			800 00
		Voucher No. 31			

On September 15, services were performed for a customer, John Smith, who was charged $150. We received $50 and he charged the balance, $100. This transaction illustrates a COMPOUND ENTRY, where two accounts are debited and one account is credited. Notice, however, that the debit amounts equal the credit. The other entries illustrated are SIMPLE entries—one debit equal to one credit.

The entry on September 20 is for $800 worth of equipment purchased on account from the Regional Supply Company. This is called a CHARGE purchase, as opposed to a cash purchase. (Accounts Payable could have been credited in this entry; however, it is preferable to show the creditor's balance in an account with an identifiable name.)

Notice that the debit account is always listed first in each journal entry. The account to be credited is indented. The amounts of the debit and credit line up with the account titles. Any explanation is listed below the last account title. The name of the month, with the year, is entered once and is not repeated until the next page. Only the day number is used unless the month changes.

Journalizing

Journalizing *begins with the source document.* The information on it tells the bookkeeping clerk all that is needed for the entry—the date, the names of the accounts to debit and credit, the amount, and, if needed, a brief explanation. Here, for example, is a check stub:

NO. 173 Oct. 1 19 9–
TO Ace Realty
FOR Oct. Rent
AMOUNT 500.00

BAL.	6	253	15
THIS CK.		500	00
BAL.	5	753	15

The entry to record this transaction in a general journal is:

JOURNAL Page 8

Date		Account Title	PR	Debit	Credit
199– Oct.	1	Rent Expense		500 00	
		Cash			500 00
		Check No. 173			

Learn the rules of how accounts increase and decrease in order to properly debit and credit accounts. Knowing these rules simplifies the entire journalizing procedure.

YOU SHOULD REMEMBER

Journal entries are listed *chronologically*.
Debit accounts and amounts are always *listed first* in journal entries.
Credit accounts and amounts *are indented following debits*.
A brief explanation ends a journal entry.
In every entry *debits equal credits*.

KNOW YOUR VOCABULARY

Use each of the following words or terms in a statement relating to bookkeeping/accounting:

Book of original entry
Chronological order
Compound entry
Direct ledger
Journal
Simple entry
Voucher

QUESTIONS

1. If there are 250 transactions in one month, at least how many entries will there probably be in a *ledger* that month?
2. Why would a numbering or lettering system not be practical in recording entries directly in a ledger?
3. Why is a journal similar to a diary?
4. How does the journal entry identify the debit(s) part of any entry compared to the credit part?

PROBLEMS

6–1 Using a general journal, page 7, record each of these transactions for Rose Klein, owner of a dress designing business:

October 2, Paid employee's salary, $175
7, Received $600 cash for a design
14, Paid $200 cash for supplies and material
16, Borrowed $1,000 cash from the Veron Trust Co.
21, Received $500 cash for a design
23, Bought a new $360 drawing table (equipment) from the Textile Equipment Company. Paid $160 cash and charged the balance, $200.
30, Withdrew $400 cash for personal use
31, Received $100 cash from Mary Wu, a customer (who bought a design last month for $350 and was charged that amount then)

6–1

GENERAL JOURNAL Page

Date		Account Title	PR	Debit	Credit

6–2 What would be a typical source document for each of the transactions listed in Problem 6–1?

THINK IT OVER

Simon Bredhoff has been using the direct ledger method in his bookkeeping records. His business activity has been increasing in recent months. Exactly what should Bredhoff do in order to maintain better control, giving him a more immediate and continuous set of information, and allowing him to follow his business activities day by day?

Ethel Cosmos keeps a ledger and a general journal for her professional consulting business. As each transaction occurs, she wonders which would be the wiser action:

(1) to enter debits and credits in accounts to keep account balances up to date, or

(2) to journalize each transaction first, to keep a running record.

What help can you offer Cosmos in making a decision that will help her follow her business in a more logical way? Which logically comes first: the journal or the ledger?

WORDS TO REMEMBER

Cross Referencing a bookkeeping procedure in which the *journal entry posting reference* column *indicates the account number* that has been posted, and the *account posting reference* column *indicates the journal page number* of the original entry

Footings tiny *pencil totals* of two or more figures in any column

Posting the procedure of *transferring entries from the journal to the ledger*

Trial Balance a two-column listing of all *ledger accounts* and their *balances*; if *debits equal credits*, the trial balance is *in balance*

CHAPTER 

POSTING THE GENERAL JOURNAL

The system of recording transactions in a general journal does not replace the use of ledger accounts. At some point, each *amount* debited or credited in the journal must be transferred to the ledger account named in the journal entry. This step is called POSTING. Posting should be done on a regular—daily, weekly, or monthly—basis, depending on the frequency of transactions.

Posting Procedure

Every ledger account must be numbered. Each one appears on a separate page or card with a number that identifies the type of account:

Classification	Account Number
Assets	11–19
Liabilities	21–29
Owner's Equity	31–39
Revenue	41–49
Expenses	51–59

If more accounts are needed in any classification, the entire ledger must be renumbered in the hundreds: 111–199; 211–299; 311–399; 411–499; 511–599.

JOURNAL TO LEDGER

The steps in posting a journal entry are as follows:

(1) Enter, for the account debited, the *amount* on the debit side of that account: - — - — (see illustration below).
(2) Enter the date—year, month, and day (thereafter, do not repeat the year and month): — — — .
(3) Enter the *journal* page number in the Posting Reference (PR) column of the account: ▪▪▪▪▪▪▪▪▪▪▪▪▪ .
(4) Enter the *account number* in the Posting Reference (PR) column of the journal: ▬▬▬▬▬ .

Repeat the posting procedure for the next account listed in the journal. Continue with each journal entry, posting debits and credits to each of the accounts listed. If the work of posting is interrupted, the bookkeeping clerk will always know exactly where to resume work—after the last posting reference *account number* in the journal PR column.

Just as debits must equal credits in each journal entry, debits must equal credits when posted to ledger accounts. The following journal entry will be posted to the accounts involved. (Assume that cash has an $800 debit balance (✓) from the preceding month.)

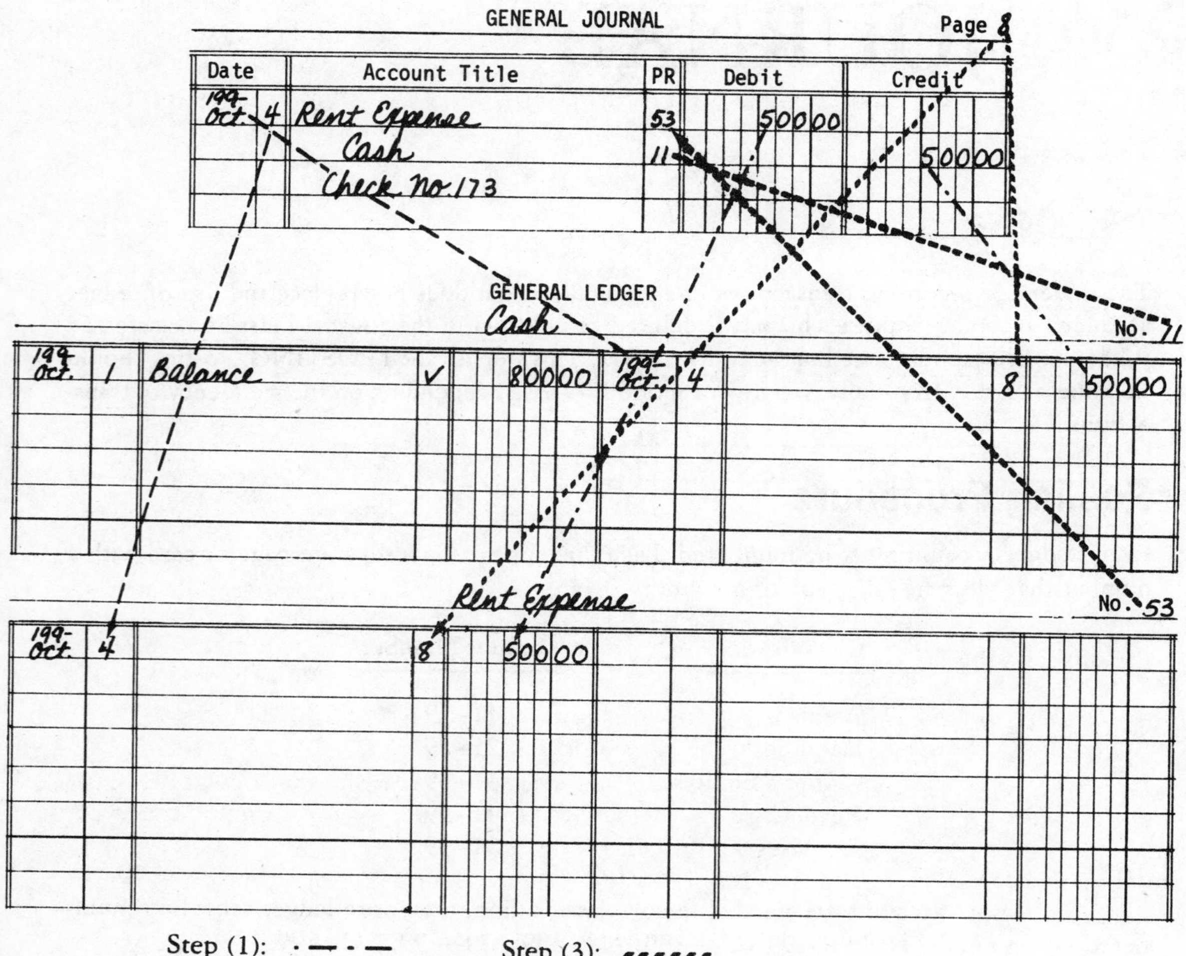

GENERAL JOURNAL
Page 8
Date
Account Title
PR
Debit
Credit
199-
Oct. 4
Rent Expense
53
500 00
Cash
11
500 00
Check No. 173
GENERAL LEDGER
Cash
No. 11
199-
Oct. 1
Balance
✓
800 00
199-
Oct. 4
8
500 00
Rent Expense
No. 53
199-
Oct. 4
8
500 00

Step (1): - — - —
Step (2): — — —
Step (3): ▪▪▪▪▪▪
Step (4): ▬▬▬▬▬

CROSS REFERENCING

It is now possible to tie together quickly the debit and credit for each transaction. Posting references refer to each other—the journal to the account number, the account to the journal page number. This is called CROSS REFERENCING. It makes the work of checking the records much simpler.

The bookkeeping process starts with the source document for a transaction. A journal entry is then recorded. The entry is posted to ledger accounts:

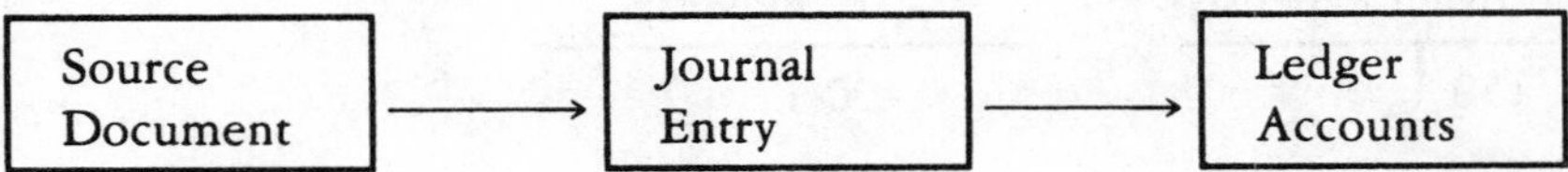

Trial Balance

When all journalizing and posting have been completed at the end of a fiscal period, or at the end of a month, the bookkeeping clerk makes a check on the accuracy of that work. A listing is made of all ledger accounts and their balances; this is called a TRIAL BALANCE.

In preparing a trial balance, the following steps are taken:

(1) Find the balance of each account, using pencil. Total all debits and credits; these are written below the last figure on each side. This is called FOOTING the ledger, and the totals are called *pencil footings.*

(2) Subtract the smaller footing from the larger (on scrap paper). In pencil, write the difference, or BALANCE of the account, on the *larger side* in the item column. Accounts will normally have balances (debit or credit) on their *increase* sides—assets are debits, liabilities are credits, owner's equity (capital) is a credit, revenue is a credit, and expenses are debits.

Supplies — No. 16

199- Oct.	2		5	100 00	199- Oct.	28		9	20 00
	14		7	50 00					
	30		10	35 00					
		165.00		185 00					

Above is a typical account that has pencil footings and a balance. Since only one credit is posted, there is no need to total that side of the account. This account, an asset, has a debit balance of $165.00.

(3) Start the trial balance with a heading to answer the questions WHO, WHAT, and WHEN.

(4) List all accounts by name in their numerical order. Each account balance is placed in either the first (debit) or second (credit) money column (see page 48).

(5) Finally, total each column. If all work is done correctly, the totals should be equal. Once again debits equal credits. The trial balance is said to be IN BALANCE. Double-rule the totals to show that the work has been completed.

Following is a ledger of simple T-account balances:

Cash		Equipment		Supplies	
2500		5000		300	

Accounts Payable		De Van Loc, Capital		Rent Income	
	1200		5150		2000

Advertising Expense		Salary Expense	
150		400	

At the end of the fiscal period (October 31) the bookkeeping clerk will prepare a trial balance of the general ledger, following the five steps listed above.

De Van Loc Company
Trial Balance
October 31, 199-

Account Title	Acct. No.	Debit	Credit
Cash		2500 00	
Equipment		5000 00	
Supplies		300 00	
Accounts Payable			1200 00
De Van Loc, Capital			5150 00
Rent Income			2000 00
Advertising Expense		150 00	
Salary Expense		400 00	
		8350 00	8350 00

YOU SHOULD REMEMBER

Account *balances* normally appear on the debit or credit side on which *the account increases.*
A trial balance *proves* the *equality of debits and credits in the ledger.*

KNOW YOUR VOCABULARY

- Balance
- Cross referencing
- Footings
- In balance
- Posting
- Trial balance

QUESTIONS

1. What steps are followed in posting journal entries?
2. On which side of accounts are balances normally found?
3. a) What does the journal posting refer to?
   b) What does the account posting refer to?
4. A bookkeeping clerk resumes his/her posting work after returning from lunch. How will he/she know where to resume?
5. What does a trial balance "in balance" prove?

PROBLEMS

7–1 Post the following entries from the general journal to the ledger accounts:

GENERAL JOURNAL Page 6

Date		Description	PR	Debit	Credit
199- Oct.	1	Equipment		1 000 00	
		Landers Mfg. Co.			1 000 00
		5 Motors, Voucher No. 31			
	10	Cash		2 500 00	
		Service Income			2 500 00
		Receipts Nos. 1-35, to date			
	18	L. D. Berger, Drawing		500 00	
		Cash			500 00
		Withdrawal, Personal Use,			
		Check No. 57			
	25	Landers Mfg. Company		250 00	
		Cash			250 00
		Partial Payment, Check No. 58			

(A partial ledger is shown here.)

Cash — No. 11

Date		Item	P.R.	Debit	Date		Item	P.R.	Credit
199- Oct.	1	Balance	✓	1750 00					

Equipment — No. 12

Date		Item	P.R.	Debit	Date		Item	P.R.	Credit
199- Oct.	1	Balance	✓	3000 00					

Landers Mfg. Company — No. 21

Date		Item	P.R.	Debit	Date		Item	P.R.	Credit

L.D. Berger, Drawing — No. 32

Date		Item	P.R.	Debit	Date		Item	P.R.	Credit

Service Income — 41

Date		Item	P.R.	Debit	Date		Item	P.R.	Credit

7–2 Below, in T-account form, is the general ledger for Harold Kriss, who operates a computer consulting firm:

Cash No. 11

Debit	Credit
1500 00	100 00
750 00	50 00
495 00	75 00
	500 00

Equipment No. 12

Debit	Credit
3500 00	
465 00	

Supplies No. 13

Debit	Credit
60 00	

Hi-Tech Company No. 21

Debit	Credit
75 00	2000 00

Comp-Software Company No. 22

Debit	Credit
	465 00

Harold Kriss, Capital No. 31

Debit	Credit
	3060 00

Harold Kriss, Drawing No. 32

Debit	Credit
500 00	

Services Income No. 41

Debit	Credit
	750 00
	495 00

Advertising Expense No. 51

Debit	Credit
100 00	

Utilities Expense No. 52

Debit	Credit
50 00	

(1) Pencil-foot the ledger to find the balance of each account.
(2) Prepare a trial balance, using today's date.

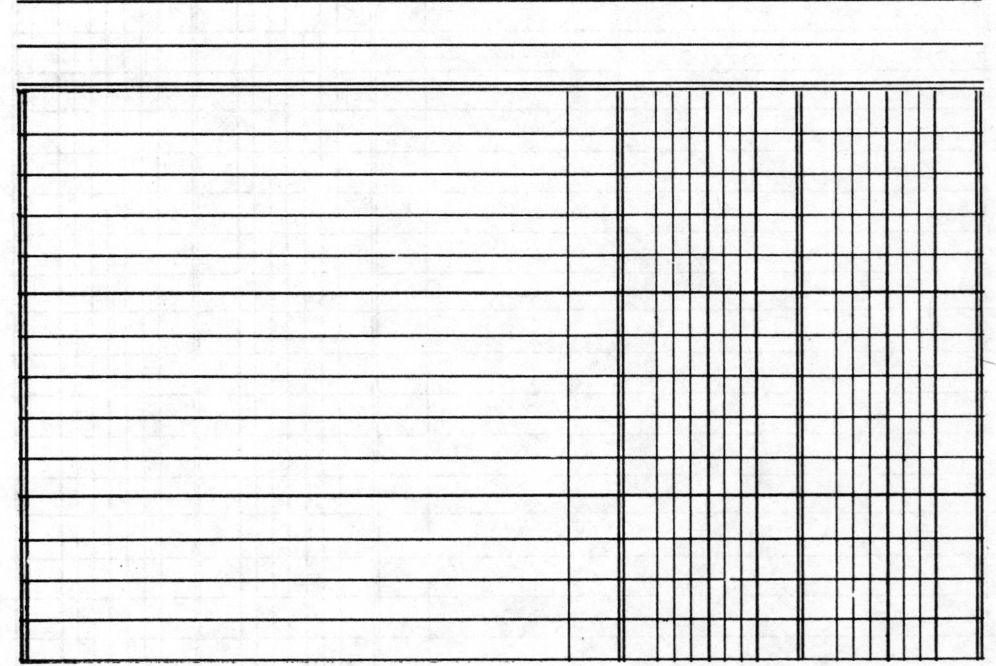

7–3 Anita Schaffer runs knitting and sewing classes from her home. Last month she completed the following transactions:

October 2, Bought class supplies for cash, $125
7, Received class fees, $200
11, Made a $50 payment to Jessup Bank due on loan
21, Received class fees, $240
27, Paid $65 for miscellaneous expenses
31, Withdrew for personal use, $300

(1) Record the transactions above in Schaffer's journal.
(2) Post the journal entries to Schaffer's ledger accounts.
(3) Foot the ledger accounts, indicating the balances at the end of the month.
(4) Prepare a trial balance, dated October 31, 199–.

(1) GENERAL JOURNAL Page 3

Date		Account Title	PR	Debit	Credit

(2) and (3)

Cash No. 11

Date		Item	PR	Debit	Date		Item	PR	Credit
199- Oct.	1	Balance	✓	1375 00					

Equipment No. 12

Date		Item	PR	Debit	Date		Item	PR	Credit
199- Oct.	1	Balance	✓	1642 50					

Supplies No. 13

Date		Item	PR	Debit	Date		Item	PR	Credit
199- Oct.	1	Balance	✓	230 00					

Jessup Bank No. 21

Date		Item	PR	Debit	Date		Item	PR	Credit
					199- Oct.	1	Balance	✓	875 00

Anita Schaffer, Capital No. 31

Date		Item	PR	Debit	Date		Item	PR	Credit
					199- Oct.	1	Balance	✓	2372 50

Anita Schaffer, Drawing No. 32

Date		Item	PR	Debit	Date		Item	PR	Credit

Fee Income No. 41

Date		Item	PR	Debit	Date		Item	PR	Credit

Miscellaneous Expense No. 51

Date		Item	PR	Debit	Date		Item	PR	Credit

(4)

THINK IT OVER

Dina Fowler has prepared a trial balance for her business. It is not in balance. She asks you where she should review her bookkeeping work, in order to find the reason. What suggestions will you make?

Ira Jacobs has prepared a trial balance that is in balance. On reviewing one entry, however, he discovers that he omitted another entry for a payment of $50 for an expense. Why did this error, or omission, not affect the equality of debits and credits in his ledger?

Can you suggest any other kinds of errors that might not cause a trial balance to be "out of balance"?

WORDS TO REMEMBER

In Balance refers to a trial balance with *equal column totals*

Out of Balance refers to a trial balance with *unequal column totals*

Work Sheet a multicolumn ruled form used to analyze a trial balance in order to prepare financial statements

THE TRIAL BALANCE AND WORK SHEET

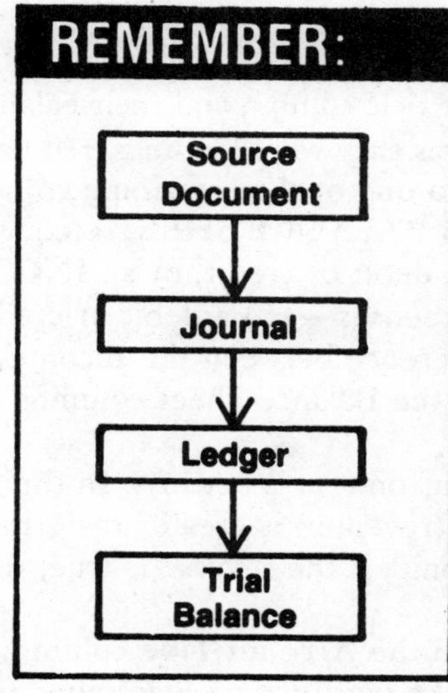

Locating Errors

A trial balance taken at the time interval desired—end of month, fiscal period, year—is a test of the equality of the debit and credit balances in the ledger. If, however, a trial balance is OUT OF BALANCE, the following steps—in reverse order—should be taken to determine the reason(s):

(1) Re-add the columns of the trial balance; perhaps they were totaled incorrectly.

(2) Examine each account balance in the trial balance, and compare these account balances to the ledger account balances. Perhaps they were carried forward incorrectly, or perhaps an account was omitted, listed twice, or placed in the wrong amount column of the trial balance (reversing a debit or a credit).

(3) Re-foot the ledger accounts to verify each account balance.

(4) If an error is not located at this point, compare each entry in the account with the original debit and credit recorded in the journal entry.

When an error is discovered in the ledger, neatly cross out the incorrect entry and write the correction above it. Never erase ink amounts or mark through an error in any way that causes the first figure to be altered. This could cause legal problems, inasmuch as bookkeeping/accounting records are legal documents.

Errors That the Trial Balance Does Not Reveal

Not all errors show up in a trial balance. The following errors do not affect the equality of debits and credits in the ledger:

(1) Omitting an entire entry.
(2) Posting to an incorrect account—a debit to another debit, a credit to another credit.
(3) Using an incorrect amount in a journal entry and posting that amount to ledger accounts.
(4) Recording a transaction twice.

The Six-Column Work Sheet

By the end of a fiscal period, the owner of a business wants the answer to a very important question: What was the net income or net loss for that period? To answer that question, a WORK SHEET is prepared. A work sheet is a ruled form of analysis paper with several columns. Because it is not part of the permanent records, however, it can be completed in pencil. The steps taken to complete a work sheet are as follows:

(1) Write a heading that answers the questions WHO, WHAT, and WHEN. The "when" part indicates the fiscal period *ending date.*
(2) List all ledger accounts in the Account title column and their balances in the first pair of money columns, arranged as they would be in a trial balance.
(3) Extend the balance of each account to one of the remaining columns by determining whether the account is a BALANCE SHEET account—assets, liabilities, and owner's equity—and a debit or credit, or an INCOME STATEMENT account—revenue, expenses—and a debit or credit.
(4) Total all remaining columns; the difference between the Income Statement columns and the difference between the Balance Sheet columns should be equal.
(5) Determine whether there was a net income or a net loss. In the Income Statement *column totals*, if the credit (revenue) is greater than the debit (expenses), there has been a net income; if the reverse is true, there has been a net loss.
(6) Identify the net income or net loss in the Account Title column; the amount is entered in the smaller of the two Income Statement and Balance Sheet columns; equal totals are then entered in each pair of columns and they are double ruled.

Examine carefully the completed work sheet on page 57. It begins with the trial balance completed for the De Van Loc Company, illustrated in Chapter 7, page 48. Note the heading (1), the trial balance (2), extending the account balances (3), totaling the last four columns and finding the difference (4), determining the amount of net income (5), and adding it to the lesser amount in both the income statement and balance sheet totals to make them equal, then double ruling (6).

De Van Loc Company
Work Sheet
For the Month Ended October 31, 199–

Account Title	A. N.	Trial Balance Debit	Trial Balance Credit	Income Statement Debit	Income Statement Credit	Balance Sheet Debit	Balance Sheet Credit
Cash	11	2500 00				2500 00	
Equipment	12	5000 00				5000 00	
Supplies	13	300 00				300 00	
Accounts Payable	21		1200 00				1200 00
De Van Loc, Capital	31		5150 00				5150 00
Rent Income	41		2000 00		2000 00		
Advertising Expense	51	150 00		150 00			
Salary Expense	52	400 00		400 00			
		8350 00	8350 00	550 00	2000 00	7800 00	6350 00
Net Income				1450 00			1450 00
				2000 00	2000 00	7800 00	7800 00

YOU SHOULD REMEMBER

Clear up all errors revealed in a trial that is out of balance *before extending* items on a work sheet.

Differences in column totals in each statement (income statement and balance sheet) on the work sheet *should be equal.*

KNOW YOUR VOCABULARY

- Balance sheet
- Income statement
- Net income
- Net loss
- Out of balance
- Work sheet

QUESTIONS

1. What is the order in which work will be checked to find an error in the trial balance?
2. What errors will cause a trial balance to be out of balance?
3. What errors can be made that will not cause a trial balance to be out of balance?
4. How is the net income or net loss for the fiscal period determined on the work sheet?

PROBLEMS

8–1 T. R. Price is a carpenter who receives a commission for odd jobs in his neighborhood. His bookkeeping records indicate the following balances (shown in T-account form):

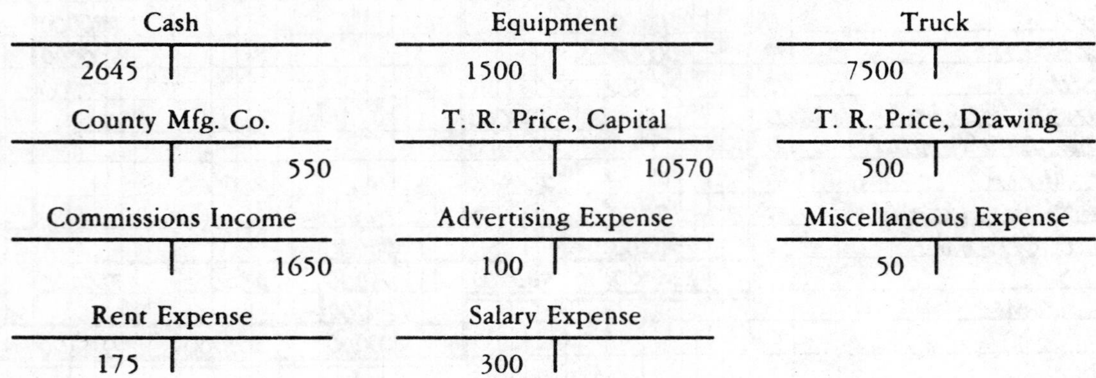

Account	Debit	Credit
Cash	2645	
Equipment	1500	
Truck	7500	
County Mfg. Co.		550
T. R. Price, Capital		10570
T. R. Price, Drawing	500	
Commissions Income		1650
Advertising Expense	100	
Miscellaneous Expense	50	
Rent Expense	175	
Salary Expense	300	

Complete a six-column work sheet for the month ended November 30, 199–. (Save your work for future problems.)

Account Title	A. N.	Trial Balance Debit	Trial Balance Credit	Income Statement Debit	Income Statement Credit	Balance Sheet Debit	Balance Sheet Credit

8–2 Below is a trial balance for Ann Danziger; however, it contains an error.

Danziger Designs
Trial Balance
September 30, 199-

	Debit	Credit
Cash	1762 50	
Accounts Receivable	738 90	
Equipment	2605 00	
Supplies	395 00	
Accounts Payable	600 00	
Ann Danziger, Capital		4251 40
Ann Danziger, Drawing	800 00	
Fees Income		2400 00
Advertising Expense	160 00	
Insurance Expense	40 00	
Materials Expense	100 00	
Rent Expense	250 00	
Salary Expense	400 00	

(1) Find the error, correcting the trial balance.

(2) Total the trial balance.

(3) What is Danziger's net income for this period?
(Complete the worksheet on the next page.)

(3) Complete the work sheet for the quarter year ended September 30. (Save your work for future problems.)

Account Title	A. N.	Trial Balance Debit	Trial Balance Credit	Income Statement Debit	Income Statement Credit	Balance Sheet Debit	Balance Sheet Credit

8–3 Rebecca Gayle operates a message delivery service. Her trial balance for the month ended October 31, 199–, is shown below:

Gayle's Reliable Service
Trial Balance
October 31, 199–

Cash	760 00	
Accounts Receivable	142 50	
Automobile	9200 00	
Supplies	350 00	
County Bank & Trust Co.		3600 00
Rebecca Gayle, Capital		6302 00
Rebecca Gayle, Drawing	600 00	
Service Income	1875 50	
Advertising Expense	200 00	
Auto Expense	400 00	
Miscellaneous Expense	50 00	
Telephone Expense	75 00	

(1) Find the error, correcting the trial balance.

(2) Complete the work sheet. (Save your work for future problems.)

Account Title	A. N.	Trial Balance		Income Statement		Balance Sheet	
		Debit	Credit	Debit	Credit	Debit	Credit

THINK IT OVER

Damien Spyridon's trial balance is not in balance. He checks his work and finds two errors. An expense account with a $100 balance was listed on the trial balance as a credit. The other error is found when he checks his posting. A journal entry amount was $54; he posted the debit as $45. Why did the trial balance columns differ by $209?

WORDS TO REMEMBER

Capital Statement a financial statement that shows how owner's equity has changed during a fiscal period

Income Statement a financial statement listing all revenue and expenses for a fiscal period, leading to the net income or net loss; a statement that describes the operations of a business over a period of time

CHAPTER 9 FINANCIAL STATEMENTS

REMEMBER:

***A, L, OE* are Balance Sheet Accounts.**

***R, E* are Income Statement Accounts.**

Because the work sheet can be completed easily and conveniently in pencil, all errors up to that point probably will have been corrected. Using the work sheet, the bookkeeping/accounting clerk prepares financial statements more formally. These will become part of the permanent records of a business.

Income Statement—Form and Content

An INCOME STATEMENT is prepared first, using the information in the Income Statement columns of the work sheet. The heading will answer the questions WHO, WHAT, and WHEN. All revenue is listed first, and totaled. Expenses are then listed, totaled, and subtracted from total revenue. The difference is the same net income (or net loss) as shown on the work sheet.

Revenue − Expenses = Net Income or Net Loss

Follow this illustration (based on the work sheet on page 57).

De Van Loc Company
Income Statement
For the Month Ended October 31, 199-

Revenue:		
Rent Income		2000 00
Expenses:		
Advertising Expense	150 00	
Salary Expense	400 00	
Total Expenses		550 00
Net Income		1450 00

If expenses are greater than revenue, the difference (revenue subtracted from expenses) is identified as a net loss. Note that the first money column is used to list more than one item; the second money column is for totals (or a single item) and the results of the business operations for the fiscal period—net income or net loss. Double lines are ruled through both money columns to show a completed statement.

Capital Statement

The next financial statement to be prepared is a CAPITAL STATEMENT. This shows how owner's equity has changed during a fiscal period. It starts with the *beginning* capital account balance. Any changes that occur are then listed. Possible changes in owner's equity are:

Increases	Decreases
(1) additional investments	(1) withdrawals
(2) net income for period	(2) net loss for period

De Van Loc's capital statement is a simple one; only two items are involved.

De Van Loc Company
Capital Statement
For the Month Ended October 31, 199-

Beginning Balance, Oct. 1, 199-		5150 00
Plus: Net Income		1450 00
Ending Balance, Oct. 31, 199-		6600 00

Following are illustrations of capital statements with more changes (headings are omitted here):

Beginning Balance, Sept. 1, 199-			7500 00
Plus: Additional Investment		1000 00	
Net Income		2500 00	
		3500 00	
Less: Withdrawals		1500 00	
Net Increase in Capital			2000 00
Ending Balance, Sept. 30, 199-			9500 00

With decreases less than increases, there is a *net increase* in capital. Always verify whichever one there is before writing the words "Net Increase" or "Net Decrease." (If withdrawals are greater than any additional investment, there may still be a net decrease—assuming a net income that does not make up the difference.)

Beginning Balance, Nov. 1, 199-			12500 00
Plus: Additional Investment		3000 00	
Less: Withdrawals	1,500 00		
Net Loss	2,000 00	3500 00	
Net Decrease in Capital			500 00
Ending Balance, Nov. 30, 199-			12000 00

Balance Sheet—Form and Content

The next financial statement to be prepared is one that was discussed in Chapter 3—a balance sheet. The information is found in the Balance Sheet columns of the work sheet, *except for owner's equity*. The capital *at the end of the fiscal period* is the ending balance found on the capital statement.

De Van Loc Company
Balance Sheet
October 31, 199—

Assets		Liabilities	
Cash	2500 00	Accounts Payable	1200 00
Equipment	5000 00	Owner's Equity	
Supplies	300 00	De Van Loc, Cap, Oct. 31	6600 00
Total Assets	7800 00	Total Liab. + O.E.	7800 00

Compare De Van Loc's capital with the amount listed on his capital statement, page 64. These two items will always agree.

YOU SHOULD REMEMBER

When *revenue is greater than expenses* there is a *net income.*
When *expenses are greater than revenue* there is a net loss.
Owner's equity is *increased* by:
—additional investments and
—net income.
Owner's equity is *decreased* by:
—withdrawals by the owner and
—net loss.

KNOW YOUR VOCABULARY

Balance sheet
Income statement
Capital statement

QUESTIONS

1. From which source of information are financial statements prepared?
2. In what order should statements be prepared?
3. What are the causes for an increase in owner's equity?
4. What are the causes for a decrease in owner's equity?
5. Why is the work sheet capital balance not used in completing a balance sheet?
6. How are the dates indicated in the "when" part of each statement's heading?

PROBLEMS

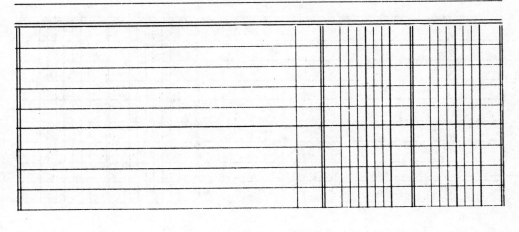

9–1 Using the completed work sheet in Problem 8–1 for T. R. Price, complete the following:

a) An income statement.
b) A capital statement.
c) A balance sheet.

a)

b)

c)

9–2 Using the completed work sheet in Problem 8–2 for Danziger Designs, complete the following:

a) An income statement.
b) A capital statement.
c) A balance sheet.

a)

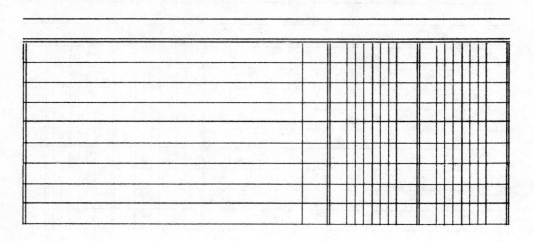

b)

c)

9–3 Using the completed work sheet in Problem 8–3 for Rebecca Gayle, complete the following:

a) An income statement.
b) A capital statement.
c) A balance sheet.

a)

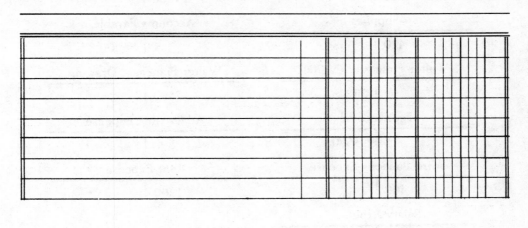

b)

c)

9–4 Below is the T-account ledger for Walter Finnegan Associates, an architectural consulting firm:

Cash	
5648	

Accounts Receivable	
2655	

Equipment	
10400	

Truck	
15000	

Supplies	
420	

Accounts Payable	
	8600

Walter Finnegan, Capital	
	28243

Walter Finnegan, Drawing	
2500	

Fees Income	
	3680

Advertising Expense	
800	

Miscellaneous Expense	
400	

Rent Expense	
1200	

Salary Expense	
1500	

(1) Complete a work sheet for the month ended November 30, 199–.

(2) Complete the following:

a) An income statement.

b) A capital statement. Assume that Finnegan's beginning capital was $25,243, and an additional $3,000 was invested during the fiscal period.

c) A balance sheet.

(1)

Account Title	A. N.	Trial Balance		Income Statement		Balance Sheet	
		Debit	Credit	Debit	Credit	Debit	Credit

2a)

2b)

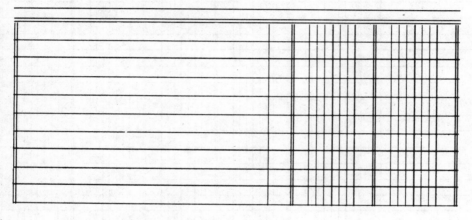

2c)

THINK IT OVER

A balance sheet has been compared to a photograph. An income statement has been compared to a moving picture. What might be the explanation for such comparisons?

WORDS TO REMEMBER

Closing entry an entry made at the end of a fiscal period to reduce an account balance to zero; to zero out an income, expense, or drawing account

Post-closing Trial Balance proof of the equality of ledger account balances, debits equal credits, *after* closing entries are posted

REMEMBER:

Investments and Revenue Increase Capital.

Withdrawals and Expenses Decrease Capital.

At the end of each fiscal period, all revenue and expense accounts and the owner's drawing account are closed. These accounts list information for a fiscal period and should not carry over to succeeding fiscal periods. Since these accounts show the changes that take place in owner's equity, their balances should be transferred to the permanent capital account in order to bring that account up to date. After being closed, these accounts can be used again, starting at a zero balance, for recording revenue, expenses, and withdrawals for the next fiscal period.

Revenue and Expense Summary

To close an account, an entry must be made which will result in posting on the opposite side of that account an amount equal to its balance. The CLOSING ENTRY procedure will reduce the balance of all revenue, expense, and drawing accounts to zero.

Revenue accounts are closed first. Since they have credit balances, they must be debited in order to have zero balances. The account credited is REVENUE AND EXPENSE SUMMARY, an owner's equity account used for special entries, including this closing procedure. This account is used to summarize the changes caused by income and expenses each fiscal period.

The second closing entry will ZERO OUT expense accounts. Since they have debit balances, they must be credited in order to have zero balances. The account debited is Revenue and Expense Summary.

The third closing entry will zero out the balance of the Revenue and Expense Summary account. The amount will always be equal to the *net income* or *net loss* for the fiscal period. If there is a net income, the summary account has a credit balance; if there is a net loss, the summary account has a debit balance. This closing entry *increases capital* for the amount of the *net income*, or *decreases capital* for the amount of the *net loss*, whichever has occurred during the fiscal period.

The following are the closing entries for the De Van Loc Company (see work sheet, page 57, Income Statement columns). These entries have been posted to the ledger accounts affected.

GENERAL JOURNAL Page 4

Date		Account Title	PR	Debit	Credit
		Closing Entries			
199- Oct.	31	Rent Income	41	2000 00	
		Revenue and Expense Summary	33		2000 00
		to close income acct.			
	31	Revenue and Expense Summary	33	550 00	
		Advertising Expense	51		150 00
		Salary Expense	52		400 00
		to close expense accts.			
	31	Revenue and Expense Summary	33	1450 00	
		De Van Loc, Capital	31		1450 00
		to close net income			

LEDGER

De Van Loc, Capital No. 31

Date		Item	PR	Debit	Date		Item	PR	Credit
					199- Oct.	1	Balance	✓	5150 00
						31		4	1450 00

Revenue and Expense Summary No. 33

Date		Item	PR	Debit	Date		Item	PR	Credit
199- Oct.	31		4	550 00	199- Oct.	31		4	2000 00
	31		4	1450 00					

Rent Income — No. 41

Date		Item	P.R.	Debit	Date		Item	P.R.	Credit
199- Oct.	31		4	2000 00	199- Oct.	15		2	1000 00
						30		3	1000 00
									2000 00

Advertising Expense — No. 51

Date		Item	P.R.	Debit	Date		Item	P.R.	Credit
199- Oct.	5		1	150 00	199- Oct.	31		4	150 00

Salary Expense — No. 52

Date		Item	P.R.	Debit	Date		Item	P.R.	Credit
199- Oct.	7		1	100 00	199- Oct.	31		4	400 00
	14		2	100 00					
	21		2	100 00					
	28		3	100 00					
				400 00					

A fourth closing entry is needed if the owner has made withdrawals during the fiscal period. Assume that John Wade's capital balance on November 30 is $12,750. His drawing account indicates withdrawals of $1,200. His net loss for the fiscal period is $500. The following are his third and fourth closing entries, which have been posted to the accounts affected.

GENERAL JOURNAL — Page 8

Date		Description	P.R.	Debit	Credit
199- Nov.	30	John Wade, Capital	31	500 00	
		Revenue and Expense Summary	33		500 00
		to close net loss			
	30	John Wade, Capital	31	1200 00	
		John Wade, Drawing	32		1200 00
		to close withdrawals			

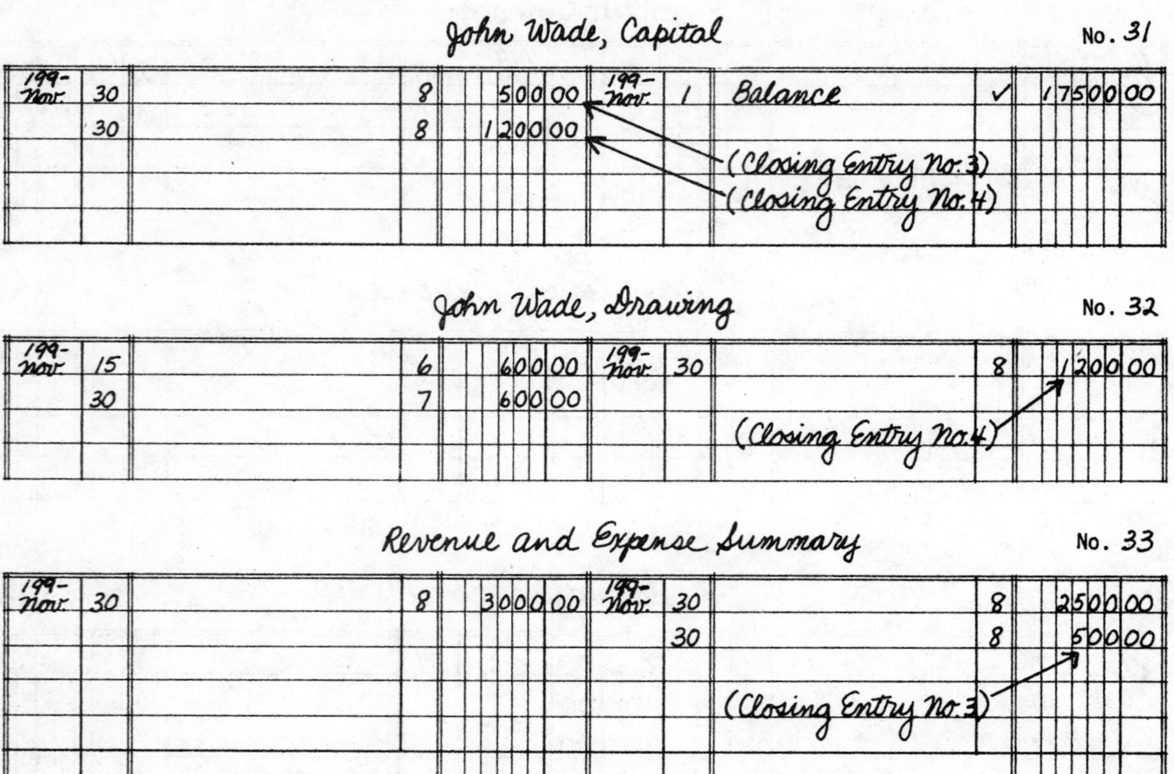

LEDGER

John Wade, Capital — No. 31

Date		Item	P.R.	Debit	Date		Item	P.R.	Credit
199- Nov.	30		8	500 00	199- Nov.	1	Balance	✓	17,500 00
	30		8	1,200 00					

(Closing Entry No. 3)
(Closing Entry No. 4)

John Wade, Drawing — No. 32

Date		Item	P.R.	Debit	Date		Item	P.R.	Credit
199- Nov.	15		6	600 00	199- Nov.	30		8	1,200 00
	30		7	600 00					

(Closing Entry No. 4)

Revenue and Expense Summary — No. 33

Date		Item	P.R.	Debit	Date		Item	P.R.	Credit
199- Nov.	30		8	3,000 00	199- Nov.	30		8	2,500 00
						30		8	500 00

(Closing Entry No. 3)

Accounts Closed/Accounts Open—Ruling, Balancing

Accounts that are closed have zero balances—all revenue, expenses, the summary account, and the drawing account. To show this clearly, they are totaled on both sides and ruled with double lines. An account that is closed and ruled is illustrated as follows.

Salary Expense — No. 517

Date		Item	P.R.	Debit	Date		Item	P.R.	Credit
199- Dec.	20		19	300 00	199- Dec.	31		22	600 00
	30		21	300 00					
				600 00					600 00

All ledger accounts, starting with the drawing account, would be ruled in this way. They have no balances; they are closed at the end of the fiscal period.

Balance sheet accounts, on the other hand, have balances that carry over to the next fiscal period. These accounts are BALANCED AND RULED. The following steps are taken:

(1) Pencil-foot the ledger—already done to take a trial balance; see page 47, steps (1) and (2).
(2) Enter in ink on the *smaller side* the amount of the account balance (√) so that both sides are equal.
(3) Write total amounts on the same line level on both debit and credit sides; double-rule the account through the date and money columns.
(4) Enter the account balance on the *larger side* as of the first day of the next fiscal period, with the word "Balance" and check mark (√) in the posting reference column.

The following are two typical accounts that have been balanced and ruled.

Cash — No. 111

Date		Item	P.R.	Debit	Date		Item	P.R.	Credit
199- Dec.	1	Balance	√	1520 00	199- Dec.	20		19	300 00
	15		17	390 00		30		21	300 00
	30		21	860 00		31	Balance	√	2170 00
		2170.00		2770 00 (pencil)					
				2770 00					2770 00
199- Jan.	1	Balance	√	2170 00					

Eleanor Smith, Capital — No. 311

Date		Item	P.R.	Debit	Date		Item	P.R.	Credit
199- Dec.	31		22	800 00	199- Dec.	1	Balance	√	15000 00
	31	Balance	√	16200 00		31		22	2000 00
							16200.00		17000 00 (pencil)
				17000 00					17000 00
					199- Jan.	1	Balance	√	16200 00

If an account has entries on one side only, it does not have to be formally balanced and ruled. Either the pencil footing or the single-entry amount stands out clearly as the balance.

Supplies — No. 115

Date		Item	P.R.	Debit	Date		Item	P.R.	Credit
199- Dec.	5		14	35 00					
	19		16	110 00					
				145 00 (pencil)					

To prove the equality of ledger debits and credits after the balancing and ruling procedure, the bookkeeping/accounting clerk prepares another trial balance—a POST-CLOSING TRIAL BALANCE. All debit account balances must equal all credit account balances. These accounts will list the same balances that are reported on the balance sheet. However, the capital account will now be updated for any net increases or net decreases that may have occurred during the fiscal period.

Compare the post-closing trial balance for De Van Loc Company with the trial balance prepared earlier (see page 48).

De Van Loc Company
Post-closing Trial Balance
October 31, 199–

		Debit	Credit
Cash		2500 00	
Equipment		5000 00	
Supplies		300 00	
Accounts Payable			1200 00
De Van Loc, Capital			6600 00
		7800 00	7800 00

A complete BOOKKEEPING/ACCOUNTING CYCLE has been illustrated in the work done to date. To complete such a cycle follow these steps carefully:

(1) Journalize transactions.
(2) Post to ledger accounts.
(3) Prepare a trial balance.
(4) Prepare a work sheet and financial statements.
(5) Make closing entries and post to accounts.
(6) Balance and rule ledger.
(7) Prepare the post-closing trial balance.

YOU SHOULD REMEMBER

The Revenue and Expense Summary account is used in closing entries *to zero out revenue and expense account balances.*

The *balance of the Revenue and Expense Summary Account* after zeroing out revenue and expense account balances *equals the net income or net loss* for the fiscal period.

After all closing entries are posted, *the Capital account* balance *equals* the amount of *owner's equity* as indicated on the capital statement and the balance sheet

KNOW YOUR VOCABULARY

Balance and rule

Bookkeeping/accounting cycle

Closing entry

Post-closing trial balance

Revenue and expense summary

Zero out

QUESTIONS

1. How are net increases and/or decreases transferred to the owner's capital account?
2. What are the four closing entries in correct order?
3. What does a credit balance in the Revenue and Expense Summary account represent?
4. What closing entry is made when the Revenue and Expense Summary account has a debit balance?
5. How is a revenue account closed?
6. How are expense accounts and the drawing account closed?
7. Which accounts remain open at the end of each fiscal period?

PROBLEMS

10–1 The following is the *partial work sheet* for Gwen Vreeland, a publishers' consultant and editor. Journalize her four closing entries at the end of the annual fiscal period *after determining the amount of her net income or net loss*. (Note that her withdrawals for the period were $1,800. This would appear in the Balance Sheet column of the work sheet.) Explanations are not needed for these entries, inasmuch as the words "Closing Entries" are written before the first one is recorded.

Account Title	A. N.	Trial Balance Debit	Trial Balance Credit	Income Statement Debit	Income Statement Credit
Cash		2000 00			
Furniture and Fixtures		5000 00			
Supplies		350 00			
Accounts Payable			1000 00		
Gwen Vreeldnd, Capital			4800 00		
Gwen Vreeland, Drawing		1800 00			
Consulting Fees Income			3750 00		3750 00
Royalty Income			500 00		500 00
Advertising Expense		100 00		100 00	
Miscellaneous Expense		60 00		60 00	
Rent Expense		250 00		250 00	
Salary Expense		400 00		400 00	
Telephone Expense		90 00		90 00	
		10050 00	10050 00	900 00	4250 00

GENERAL JOURNAL Page 18

10–2 **Below is a listing of the ledger accounts and their balances for the Allen Insurance Agency.**

Cash	**$ 800.00**
Accounts Receivable	**3,895.00**
Equipment	**4,000.00**
Automobile	**12,500.00**
Supplies	**750.00**
Accounts Payable	**6,000.00**
Elliot Allen, Capital	**12,920.00**
Elliot Allen, Drawing	**1,500.00**
Commissions Income	**6,500.00**
Automobile Expense	**600.00**
Office Expense	**175.00**
Rent Expense	**300.00**
Salary Expense	**900.00**

(1) Complete a work sheet for the month ended November 30, 199–.
(2) Journalize the four closing entries.

(1)

Account Title	A. N.	Trial Balance		Income Statement		Balance Sheet	
		Debit	Credit	Debit	Credit	Debit	Credit

(2)

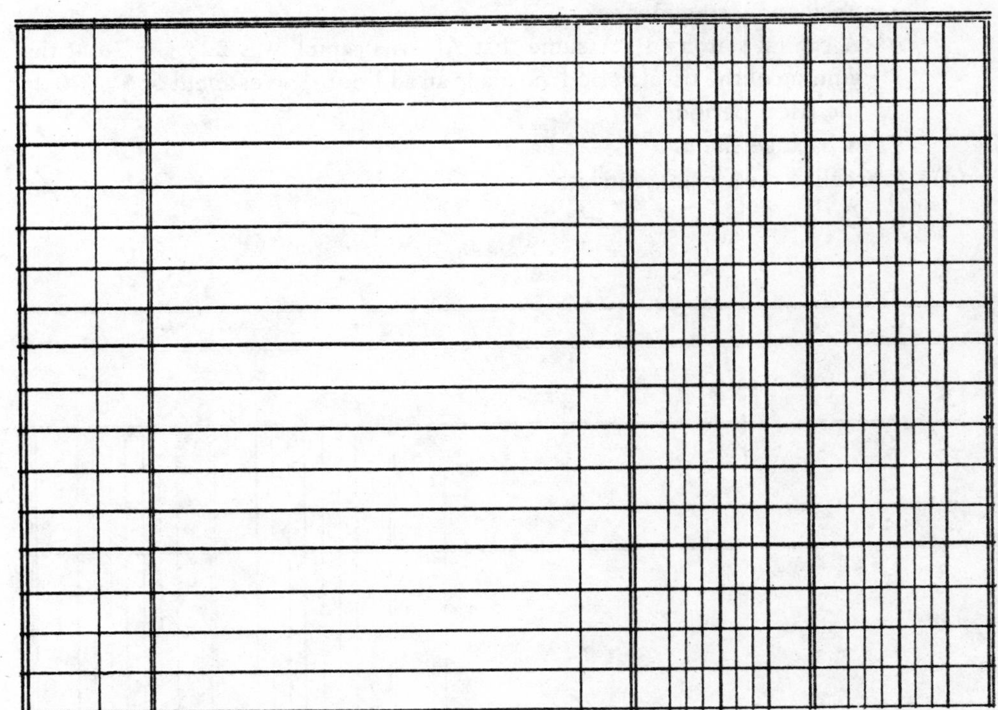

10–3 Earl Alpert, an attorney, has asked you to complete the work indicated:

(1) Complete the work sheet below.

Earl Alpert, Esquire
Work Sheet
For 3 Months Ended June 30, 199–

Account Title	A. N.	Trial Balance Debit	Trial Balance Credit	Income Statement Debit	Income Statement Credit	Balance Sheet Debit	Balance Sheet Credit
Cash	11	1605 00					
Accounts Receivable	12	14580 00					
Office Equipment	13	3960 00					
Furniture	14	5250 00					
Supplies	15	830 75					
Accounts Payable	21		1875 00				
Earl Alpert, Capital	31		24300 75				
Earl Alpert, Drawing	32	4800 00					
Legal Fees Income	41		9500 00				
Miscellaneous Expense	51	150 00					
Office Expense	52	225 00					
Rent Expense	53	1200 00					
Salary Expense	54	3000 00					
Travel Expense	55	75 00					

(2) Complete the following financial statements:

a) An income statement.

b) A capital statement. Assume that Alpert's capital was $23,300.75 at the beginning of the fiscal period; he made an additional investment of $1,000 during the fiscal period.

c) A balance sheet.

(3) Journalize the closing entries.

2a)

2b)

2c)

(3)

10–4 Pamela Washington is a recent college graduate who has started her own private accounting practice. Her journal and ledger indicate that all transactions have been posted, and she is about to complete the work of the bookkeeping/accounting cycle.

(1) Pencil-foot the ledger and take a trial balance, using the work sheet form.

(2) Complete the work sheet, and prepare the following:

a) An income statement.

b) A capital statement.

c) A balance sheet.

(3) Journalize and post the closing entries.

(4) Balance and rule the ledger.

(5) Take a post-closing trial balance.

Cash No. 11

Date		Item	P.R.	Debit	Date		Item	P.R.	Credit
199- Dec.	1	Balance	✓	1,000.00	199- Dec.	20		5	250.00
	10		4	500.00		30		5	175.00
	22		5	750.00		31		6	100.00
			6	1,350.00		31		6	90.00
						31		6	800.00

Accounts Receivable No. 12

Date		Item	P.R.	Debit	Date		Item	P.R.	Credit
199- Dec.	1	Balance	✓	2,000.00	199- Dec.	22		5	750.00

Equipment No. 13

Date		Item	P.R.	Debit	Date		Item	P.R.	Credit
199- Dec.	1	Balance	✓	3,500.00					
	15		4	1,500.00					

Supplies No. 14

Date		Item	P.R.	Debit	Date		Item	P.R.	Credit
199- Dec.	1	Balance	✓	580.00					

Accounts Payable

No. 21

Date		Item	P.R.	Debit	Date		Item	P.R.	Credit
199- Dec.	20		5	250 00	199- Dec.	1	Balance	✓	450 00
						15		4	1500 00

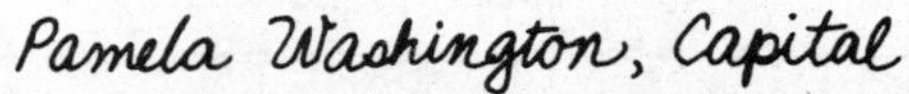

No. 31

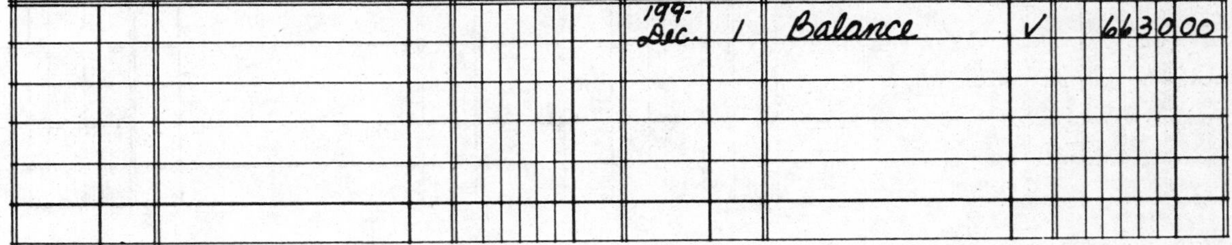

Date		Item	P.R.	Debit	Date		Item	P.R.	Credit
					199- Dec.	1	Balance	✓	6630 00

Pamela Washington, Drawing

No. 32

Date		Item	P.R.	Debit	Date		Item	P.R.	Credit
199- Dec.	31		6	800 00					

Revenue and Expense Summary

No. 33

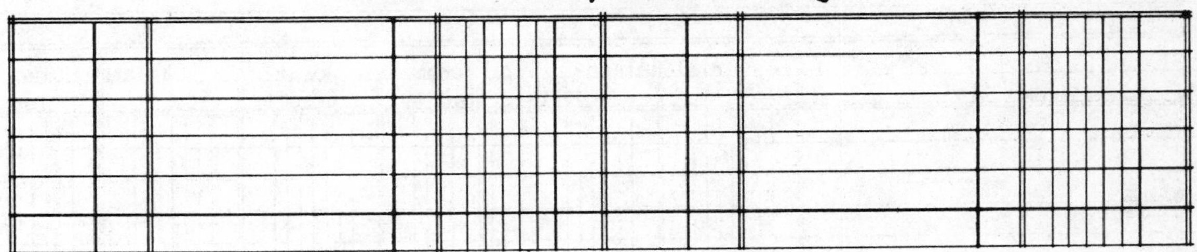

Fees Income

No. 41

Date		Item	P.R.	Debit	Date		Item	P.R.	Credit
					199- Dec.	10		4	500 00
						31		6	1350 00

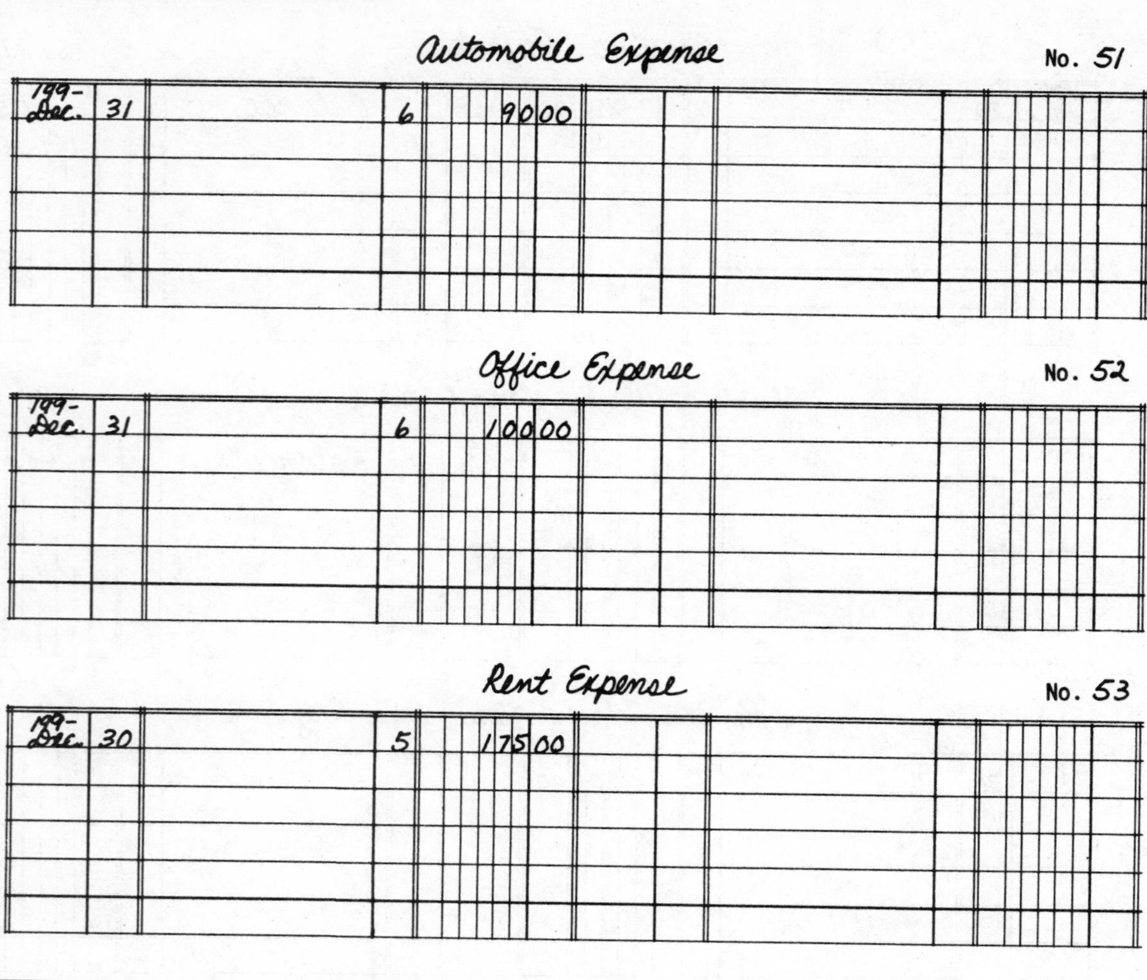

Automobile Expense — No. 51

Date			P.R.	Debit			P.R.	Credit
199- Dec.	31		6	90 00				

Office Expense — No. 52

Date			P.R.	Debit			P.R.	Credit
199- Dec.	31		6	100 00				

Rent Expense — No. 53

Date			P.R.	Debit			P.R.	Credit
199- Dec.	30		5	175 00				

Account Title	A. N.	Trial Balance Debit	Trial Balance Credit	Income Statement Debit	Income Statement Credit	Balance Sheet Debit	Balance Sheet Credit

Pamela Washington
Income Statement
For the Month Ended December 31, 199–

Pamela Washington
Capital Statement
For the Month Ended December 31, 199–

Pamela Washington
Balance Sheet
December 31, 199–

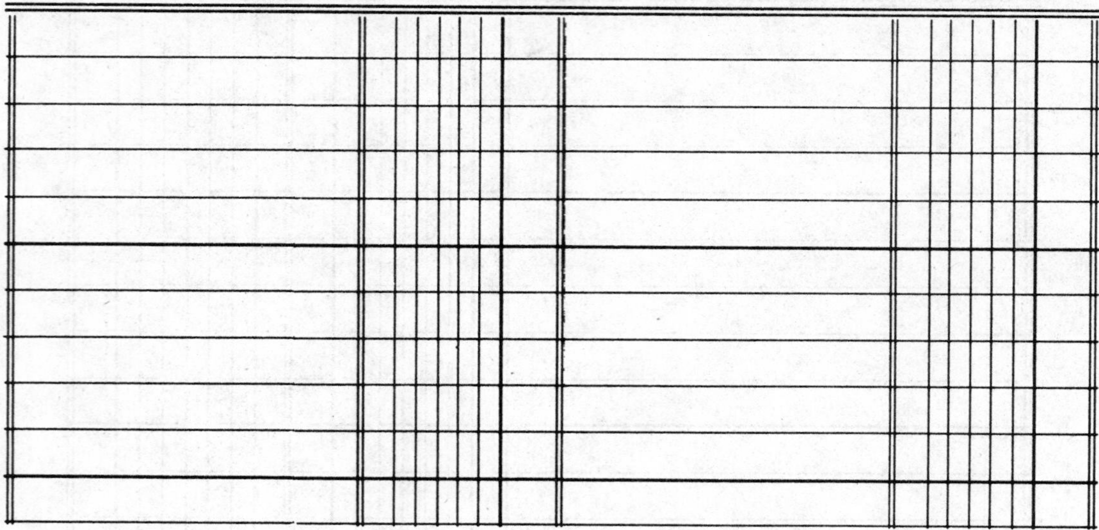

GENERAL JOURNAL Page 7

Date		Account Title	PR	Debit	Credit

Pamela Washington
Post-closing Trial Balance
December 31, 199-

THINK IT OVER

Len Green says he does not make closing entries, nor does he ever prepare a post-closing trial balance. He claims these steps are not needed because he uses only ten to twelve accounts. What difficulties will he encounter two or three fiscal periods from now, if he wishes to prepare financial statements? Do you think the Internal Revenue Service would approve of a tax return based on statements that confuse information from one fiscal period to the next?

WORDS TO REMEMBER

Bank Reconciliation a "calculation" made to find the correct, available amount of cash on deposit in a *checking account*; adjust the *checkbook balance* and the *bank statement balance*

Drawer one who *writes a check and signs it*

Drawee *the bank* in which a *checking account is kept*

Endorsement *the payee's signature* on the back of a check

Payee the *party to whom payment* is made by check

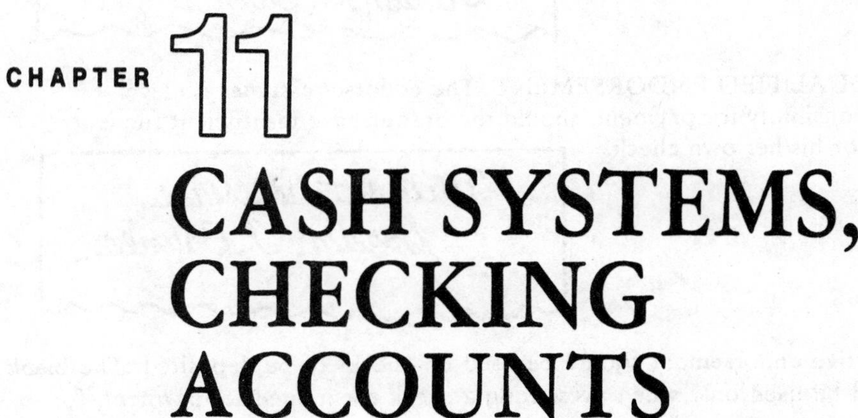

CHAPTER 11 CASH SYSTEMS, CHECKING ACCOUNTS

Most businesses make payments by checks drawn on local commercial banks. Many individuals now use checking accounts drawing on funds in savings banks and/or in money funds. A check is a written order directing the DRAWEE (the bank) to make payment to the PAYEE (the party indicated by the words "Pay to the order of") from the account balance of the DRAWER (the party who signs the order or check).

Opening a Checking Account

When a checking account is opened, each person authorized to sign checks completes a signature card. A deposit slip is used to list items to be added to the account, including checks received from others—paychecks, amounts collected from customers, and so on.

Endorsing Checks

Each check deposited must be endorsed, that is, signed on the back by the payee. There are several types of endorsements.

(1) An ENDORSEMENT IN BLANK. This is a simple signature of the depositor.

Gordon T. Barnes

(2) A SPECIAL (or FULL) ENDORSEMENT. This states to whom a check is to be paid.

Pay to the order of
Wilma Higgins
Gordon T. Barnes

(3) A RESTRICTIVE ENDORSEMENT. This limits the further purpose or use of the check.

For deposit only
Acct. No. 831456
Gordon T. Barnes

(4) A QUALIFIED ENDORSEMENT. The endorser assumes no legal responsibility for payment, should the drawer have insufficient funds to honor his/her own check.

Without recourse
Gordon T. Barnes

The restrictive endorsement should be used on checks to be deposited. The blank endorsement should be used only when presenting a check for immediate payment, for example, when cashing one's paycheck.

Making Deposits

Assume that Gordon Barnes opens a checking account and completes the following deposit slip:

FOR DEPOSIT TO THE ACCOUNT OF

NAME *Gordon T. Barnes*
ADDRESS *125 Main St. Bolton*
DATE *Jan. 2* 19*9-*

BOLTON NATIONAL BANK
New York, NY

CHECKS AND OTHER ITEMS ARE RECEIVED FOR DEPOSIT SUBJECT TO THE TERMS AND CONDITIONS OF THIS BANK'S COLLECTION AGREEMENT

	DOLLARS	CENTS
BILLS	250	00
COINS	—	
CHECKS AS FOLLOWS, PROPERLY ENDORSED		
	150	00
	500	00
	375	00
TOTAL DEPOSIT	1,275	00

⑆0860⑈0830⑆1243⑈676⑈

His account balance will be $1,275, and that amount will be entered on his check stub record on the balance brought forward (Bal. Bro't For'd) line. As future deposits are made, he will add to find the total; as checks are drawn, he will subtract to find the balance carried forward (Bal. Car'd For'd).

Drawing Checks

Follow these stubs and checks completed by Barnes for each of these cash payment transactions:

January 2, 199–, Paid Ace Realty $250 for month's rent; check No. 101
5, 199–, Paid Security National Bank $300 on loan balance; check No. 102

(Be sure stubs are completed first, showing all information; then complete each check, using pen and ink.)

NO. 101 $250.00
DATE Jan. 2 19 9–
TO Ace Realty
FOR January rent

	DOLLARS	CENTS
BAL. BRO'T FOR'D	1275	00
AMT. DEPOSITED		
TOTAL	1275	00
AMT. THIS CHECK	250	00
BAL. CAR'D FOR'D	1025	00

No 101
1-830
860

January 2 19 9–

Pay to the order of Ace Realty $ 250 00

Two hundred fifty + 00/100 Dollars

BOLTON NATIONAL BANK
of New York, NY

Gordon T. Barnes

⑆0860⑉0830⑆ 1243⑉671⑈

NO 102 $300.00
DATE Jan. 5 19 9–
TO Security National Bank
FOR loan payment

	DOLLARS	CENTS
BAL. BRO'T FOR'D	1025	00
AMT. DEPOSITED		
TOTAL	1025	00
AMT. THIS CHECK	300	00
BAL. CAR'D FOR'D	725	00

No 102
1-830
860

January 5 19 9–

Pay to the order of Security National Bank $ 300 00

Three hundred + 00/100 Dollars

BOLTON NATIONAL BANK
of New York, NY

Gordon T. Barnes

⑆0860⑉0830⑆ 1243⑉671⑈

Notice that the balance carried forward from stub No. 101 is brought forward to stub No. 102. In this way, Barnes will always have a running balance in his checking account.

Each check stub will serve as the source of information for making a journal entry. The two entries for stubs No. 101 and No. 102 are illustrated as follows.

Date		Account		Debit	Credit
199– Jan.	2	Rent Expense		250 00	
		Cash			250 00
		Check No. 101			
	5	Security National Bank		300 00	
		Cash			300 00
		Check No. 102			

The Bank Statement

At the end of the month, or at a set date during each month, the bank sends each depositor a BANK STATEMENT. This is the bank's record of the deposits made, and the checks drawn *and presented for payment*. These checks are CANCELED—marked paid—and returned to the depositor with the bank statement. If any charges have been made by the bank for handling this account, they are identified as "SC" ("service charge") and deducted from the balance. The depositor makes a similar deduction on the next check stub.

Here is the entry Barnes makes in his journal for the service charge made on his statement at the end of the month:

			Debit	Credit
	31	Miscellaneous Expense	3 75	
		Cash		3 75
		Bank Service Charge, Jan.		

Reconciling Check Stub Balance and Bank Statement

Frequently, the depositor's check stub balance and the checking account bank statement balance do not agree by the end of each month. There are several reasons for these differences.

(1) A late deposit, or a DEPOSIT IN TRANSIT, is added into the *check stub balance* but does not reach the bank in time to be recorded on the bank statement—*add any late or omitted deposits to the bank balance.*

(2) Some checks drawn and sent to distant points have not cleared back to the depositor's bank in time to be recorded on the bank statement—*subtract the amount of OUTSTANDING CHECKS from the bank balance.*

(3) If the bank made any service charges, they are deducted on the bank statement—*subtract the service charge on the check stub record.*

At this point, Barnes prepares a BANK RECONCILIATION STATEMENT to determine his correct, available checkbook and bank balance. This amount must be the same for both balances at any given time.

Gordon T. Barnes
Bank Reconciliation Statement
January 31, 199–

Checkbook Balance	675.00	Bank Balance	895.00
Deduct: Service Charge	3.75	Add: Deposit in Transit	200.00
			1095.00
		Deduct: Outstanding Checks	
		No. 119, 100.00	
		No. 120, 200.00	
		No. 121, 123.75	
			423.75
Correct Check Stub Balance	671.25	Available Bank Balance	671.25

The amount of cash that Barnes has in his checking account, against which he can draw future checks, is $671.25. If he had not prepared this reconciliation, he might have **OVERDRAWN** his account. One or more of his checks might have been dishonored because of insufficient funds.

YOU SHOULD REMEMBER
Outstanding checks *reduce* a bank statement balance.
A bank reconciliation is necessary to avoid *overdrawing* one's checking account.

KNOW YOUR VOCABULARY

- Bank reconciliation
- Bank statement
- Canceled
- Deposit in transit
- Drawee; drawer
- Endorsement in blank
- Full endorsement (special)
- Outstanding checks
- Overdrawn
- Payee
- Qualified endorsement
- Restrictive endorsement

QUESTIONS

1. Why is a check referred to as a "three-party instrument"?
2. How is a signature card used by the bank teller?
3. What entry is recorded for a bank service charge?
4. Why is a reconciliation statement necessary?

PROBLEMS

11–1 Complete Marian Moore's deposit slip for the following items:

23 twenty-dollar bills
48 ten-dollar bills
16 five-dollar bills
29 one-dollar bills
Checks: $148.65 and $79.15

18 quarters
31 dimes
14 nickels
42 pennies

FOR DEPOSIT TO THE ACCOUNT OF

NAME ______________________

ADDRESS ______________________

DATE ______________ 19__

BOLTON NATIONAL BANK
New York, NY

CHECKS AND OTHER ITEMS ARE RECEIVED FOR DEPOSIT SUBJECT TO THE TERMS AND CONDITIONS OF THIS BANK'S COLLECTION AGREEMENT

	DOLLARS	CENTS
BILLS		
COINS		
CHECKS AS FOLLOWS, PROPERLY ENDORSED		
TOTAL DEPOSIT		

⑆0860⑈0830⑆1843⑈671⑈

11–2 Louann Pringle, owner of a home cleaning service, completed the following checkbook transactions:

January 15, Paid for cleaning supplies, $40; check No. 118
19, Paid for taxi service, $15; check No. 119
22, Deposited $75 in bills
22, Withdrew $50 for personal use; check No. 120

(1) Complete each stub and check, signing each check as Pringle would.
(2) Complete the deposit slip and enter the amount on the deposit line of the last check stub.

(1)

NO.________ $________
DATE________ 19____
TO________
FOR________

	DOLLARS	CENTS
BAL. BRO'T FOR'D	136	50
AMT. DEPOSITED		
TOTAL		
AMT. THIS CHECK		
BAL. CAR'D FOR'D		

No.________
1-830/860

________19____

Pay to the order of ________ $________

________ Dollars

BOLTON NATIONAL BANK
of New York, NY

____

⑆0860⑈0830⑆ 1848⑈671⑈

NO.________ $________
DATE________ 19____
TO________
FOR________

	DOLLARS	CENTS
BAL. BRO'T FOR'D		
AMT. DEPOSITED		
TOTAL		
AMT. THIS CHECK		
BAL. CAR'D FOR'D		

No.________
1-830/860

________19____

Pay to the order of ________ $________

________ Dollars

BOLTON NATIONAL BANK
of New York, NY

____

⑆0860⑈0830⑆ 1848⑈671⑈

(2)

FOR DEPOSIT TO THE ACCOUNT OF

NAME ________

ADDRESS ________

DATE________ 19____

BOLTON NATIONAL BANK
New York, NY

CHECKS AND OTHER ITEMS ARE RECEIVED FOR DEPOSIT SUBJECT TO THE TERMS AND CONDITIONS OF THIS BANK'S COLLECTION AGREEMENT.

	DOLLARS	CENTS
BILLS		
COINS		
CHECKS AS FOLLOWS, PROPERLY ENDORSED		
TOTAL DEPOSIT		

⑆0860⑈0830⑆1848⑈671⑈

(1)

NO. ______ $ ______	
DATE ______ 19 ___	**No.** ______
TO ______	1-830 / 860
FOR ______	______ 19 ___
	Pay to the order of ______ $ ______

	DOLLARS	CENTS
BAL. BRO'T FOR'D		
AMT. DEPOSITED		
TOTAL		
AMT. THIS CHECK		
BAL. CAR'D FOR'D		

______ **Dollars**

BOLTON NATIONAL BANK
of New York, NY

⑆0860⑈0830⑆ 1848⑈671⑈

11–3 Helen Spiro's last check stub balance was $420.90. Her bank statement balance dated November 30, 198– was $397.40. A $250 deposit was in transit on that date. Outstanding checks were as follows: No. 217, $75.00; No. 219, $105.50; No. 220, $50.00. The bank service charge for the month was $4.00. Prepare a reconciliation statement, indicating the correct checkbook balance and available bank balance on November 30.

Checkbook Balance	**Bank Balance**

11–4 Yoshi Kawahara, a landscape engineer, received his January bank statement on February 2. The balance was $626.66. His last check stub balance was $708.92. On comparing the two, he noted that a deposit of $375 made on January 31 was not included on the statement; also, a bank service charge of $3.60 was deducted. Outstanding checks were as follows: No. 641, $92.50; No. 644, $107.25; No. 646, $37.80; and No. 647, $58.79.

(1) Complete a reconciliation statement, indicating Kawahara's correct, available bank balance.

(2) Record the service charge in Kawahara's general journal.

(1)

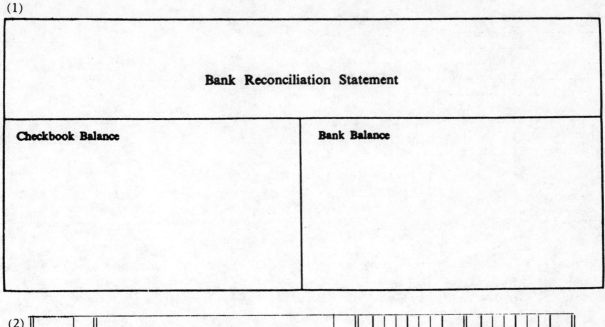

Bank Reconciliation Statement	
Checkbook Balance	**Bank Balance**

(2)

THINK IT OVER

Timothy Hankins used a qualified endorsement in cashing a check that subsequently was dishonored because of insufficient funds. What rights does the bank cashing the check have? Who is liable for payment?

WORDS TO REMEMBER

Disbursement a *payment* of cash

Petty Cash a separate cash fund used for *small disbursements* for which checks might be inappropriate

Replenish to bring the *petty cash fund up* to the *amount* at which it was originally *established*

Voucher *a special form* used to show *how much* and *to whom* petty cash has been paid, as well as *the date* and *the signature* of the party receiving the cash

THE PETTY CASH FUND

Purpose of the Fund

All cash received by a business should be deposited promptly in a checking account. Also, withdrawals are usually made by issuing checks signed by an authorized officer of the business. In that way there is a record of all funds coming in (cash debit) and all funds paid out (cash credit). However, there are times when small amounts must be paid out, perhaps for postage stamps, a collect telegram, or a package delivered collect on delivery, for which drawing a check would not be practical.

A special PETTY CASH fund is maintained for these small payments. This fund requires strict control because of the danger of missing cash. The following procedures are recommended to safeguard the petty cash fund:

(1) Petty cash should be kept separately from any other cash on hand.
(2) One person only should be held responsible for the petty cash fund.
(3) A record of each payment from petty cash should be kept, showing the person to whom it was paid, the reason, the date, the amount, and, if possible, the signature of the person to whom it was given.

Establishing the Fund

To establish a petty cash fund, a check is drawn *payable to Petty Cash*, a new ledger account, directly following the Cash account.

NO. 376 $ 40.00	**ACE TRAVEL SERVICE** No. 376
DATE August 2 19 9-	1-830 / 860
TO Petty Cash	August 2 19 9-
FOR to Establish fund	Pay to the order of Petty Cash $40.00
	Forty & 00/100 Dollars

	DOLLARS	CENTS
BAL. BRO'T FOR'D	581	36
AMT. DEPOSITED	400	00
TOTAL	981	36
AMT. THIS CHECK	40	00
BAL. CAR'D FOR'D	941	36

BOLTON NATIONAL BANK
of New York, NY

Hans Petersen

⑆0860⑈0830⑆ 1243⑈671⑈

The preceding check is endorsed by Hans Petersen and cashed. The amount is turned over to the person in charge of the fund, to be placed in a drawer or cash box, under lock and key. The check stub becomes the source document for the following journal entry:

199- Aug.	2	Petty Cash	40 00	
		Cash		40 00
		To Establish Fund, Check No. 376		

Making Disbursements

Petty cash DISBURSEMENTS are made now whenever small amounts must be paid. The person requesting the amount may be required to fill out a numbered PETTY CASH VOUCHER, giving all required information and signing the voucher. The authorized signature is then obtained to make the disbursement from the fund. The voucher is filed or kept in a separate compartment of the fund box. The following is a typical petty cash voucher:

No. ______

ACE TRAVEL SERVICE

Petty Cash Voucher

Date ____________ 19____

Pay to ____________________

For ____________________

Amount
$

________________ ________________

Payment Received Authorized

As the amount of petty cash remaining in the fund decreases, the dollar amount of the vouchers increases. At any time, the two taken together will total the ***original amount in the fund***. When the petty cash fund balance gets low, it will be **REPLENISHED** by drawing another check payable to petty cash. The amount of this check will be exactly ***equal to the total of the vouchers***. The check is cashed, and the money is placed in the petty cash drawer or box. Once again, the petty cash fund equals the total amount for which the fund was established originally.

Assume that petty cash vouchers indicate that payments were made over a period of time for many items. These vouchers are sorted out as follows:

Office expenses	$17.50	
Delivery expenses	9.60	
Miscellaneous expenses	5.95	$33.05

Proving Petty Cash

To *prove petty cash* at this point, the remaining cash is counted. Since the fund started with $40, there should be $6.95 remaining in the petty cash fund. This proves correct:

$40.00	(original balance)
− 33.05	(disbursements)
$ 6.95	(cash fund count)

The replenishing check stub and check are shown below:

NO. 387 $ 33.05
DATE August 31 19 9–
TO Petty Cash
FOR Replenish fund: Off. Supp. $17.50; Del. Exp. $9.60; Misc. Exp. $5.95

	DOLLARS	CENTS
BAL. BRO'T FOR'D	642	79
AMT. DEPOSITED		
TOTAL	642	79
AMT. THIS CHECK	33	05
BAL. CAR'D FOR'D	609	74

ACE TRAVEL SERVICE No. 387
1-830/860
August 31 19 9–
Pay to the order of Petty Cash $ 33 05/100
Thirty-three + 05/100 Dollars
BOLTON NATIONAL BANK
of New York, NY
Hans Petersen
⑆0860⑈0830⑆ 1243⑈671⑈

Replenishing the Fund

The replenishing entry prepared from the check stub will result in a debit to the various items for which petty cash has been disbursed. In that way ***the only debit to the petty cash account is from the entry to establish the fund***; that will remain the account balance, unless the fund is changed. The items for which petty cash was spent will be posted to the specific accounts for which petty cash was disbursed.

			Debit	Credit
	31	Delivery Expense	9 60	
		Miscellaneous Expense	5 95	
		Office Expense	17 50	
		Cash		33 05
		To Replenish Petty Cash,		
		Check No. 387		

Petty cash should be replenished at least once each month, usually at the end of the month, or the end of a fiscal period, and whenever the fund runs low.

YOU SHOULD REMEMBER

Only *one person* should be *responsible for a petty cash fund.*

The *sum of all vouchers* (for which disbursements have been made) *plus cash* in the petty cash fund must *equal the original amount* of the fund.

The *replenishing entry* debits the *accounts* for which petty cash was disbursed.

Only *one amount* appears as a *debit in the petty cash account—the amount* for which it was *established.*

KNOW YOUR VOCABULARY

Disbursements	Petty cash voucher
Petty cash	Replenish

QUESTIONS

1. Why is it recommended procedure to have one person in charge of the petty cash fund?
2. What is the source document for the *entry* to establish petty cash? To replenish petty cash?
3. What is the journal entry to establish petty cash?
4. What is the journal entry to replenish petty cash?
5. How is petty cash proved?

PROBLEMS

12–1 Hilda Marcello, owner of Space Travel Services, has decided to establish a petty cash fund because of frequent, small disbursements.

(1) Draw a check for $35 to establish the fund.

(2) As the authorized person, complete petty cash vouchers for each of the following disbursements:

April 2, $2.75 to messenger who delivered a package (delivery expense)
9, $8.00 for postage (office expense)
16, $10.00 gasoline for auto (auto expense)
23, $7.50 for printing business cards (miscellaneous expense)
30, $4.00 for postage

(3) Sort these vouchers; prove petty cash; complete a check stub and check to replenish the petty cash fund on the last day of the month.

NO. 138	$
DATE	19
TO	
FOR	

	DOLLARS	CENTS
BAL. BRO'T FOR'D	1406	92
AMT. DEPOSITED		
TOTAL		
AMT. THIS CHECK		
BAL. CAR'D FOR'D		

SPACE TRAVEL SERVICES

No. ______

1-830
860

______ 19 ______

Pay to the order of ______ $ ______

______ Dollars

BOLTON NATIONAL BANK
of New York, NY

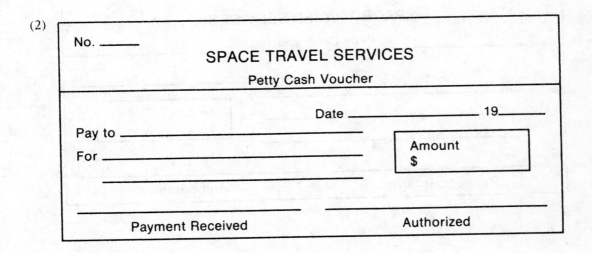

⑆0860⑈0830⑆ 1243⑈671⑈

(2)

No. ______

SPACE TRAVEL SERVICES

Petty Cash Voucher

Date ______ 19 ______

Pay to ______

For ______

Amount
$

______ Payment Received

______ Authorized

No. ______

SPACE TRAVEL SERVICES

Petty Cash Voucher

Date ______ 19 ______

Pay to ______

For ______

Amount
$

______ Payment Received

______ Authorized

No. ______

SPACE TRAVEL SERVICES

Petty Cash Voucher

Date ______________ 19____

Pay to ______________________________

For ______________________________

____

Amount
$

______________________ ______________________

Payment Received Authorized

No. ______

SPACE TRAVEL SERVICES

Petty Cash Voucher

Date ______________ 19____

Pay to ______________________________

For ______________________________

____

Amount
$

______________________ ______________________

Payment Received Authorized

No. ______

SPACE TRAVEL SERVICES

Petty Cash Voucher

Date ______________ 19____

Pay to ______________________

For ______________________

____

Amount
$

______________________ Payment Received

______________________ Authorized

3)

NO. 156	$	
DATE	19	
TO		
FOR		
	DOLLARS	CENTS
BAL. BRO'T FOR'D	1091	37
AMT. DEPOSITED	500	00
TOTAL	1591	37
AMT. THIS CHECK		
BAL. CAR'D FOR'D		

SPACE TRAVEL SERVICES

No. ______

1-315
860

______________ 19____

Pay to the order of ______________________ $ ______

______________________ Dollars

BOLTON NATIONAL BANK
of Long Island, NY

⑆0860⑈0830⑆ 1243⑈671⑈

12–2 Using the information in Problem 12–1 (1) and (3), complete the journal entries to establish the petty cash fund and to replenish it.

GENERAL JOURNAL Page 15

Date		Account Title	PR	Debit	Credit

THINK IT OVER

Connie's Interior Designs has a $50 petty cash fund. The owner's assistant, Jim Landers, is authorized to draw checks from the regular checking account and is also in charge of the petty cash fund. Last month, disbursements from the fund increased, and the fund had to be replenished several times. What recommendations might be made to the owner regarding the control factor, as well as the amount in the fund?

CYCLE ONE EXAMINATION

Part I Indicate by a check (√) in the column at the right whether each statement is TRUE or FALSE.

Statement		T	F
Example: All accounts increase by debits.			√
1. Liabilities and owner's equity increase by credits.	1.		
2. For every transaction, increases equal decreases.	2.		
3. For every transaction, debits equal credits.	3.		
4. A debit to the Cash account results in an increase.	4.		
5. A debit to J. Smith, Capital, results in an increase.	5.		
6. A journal entry is posted to ledger accounts.	6.		
7. The ledger account PR column indicates the journal page number.	7.		
8. A balance sheet describes the financial operations over a period of time.	8.		
9. An income statement is a picture of the financial condition of a business.	9.		
10. The omission of a transaction will cause a trial balance to be out of balance.	10.		
11. A $100 debit posted as a credit will cause Trial Balance columns to differ by $200.	11.		
12. A work sheet aids in the preparation of financial statements.	12.		
13. A capital statement starts with owner's equity at the end of the fiscal period.	13.		
14. Closing entries result in zero balances in revenue and expense accounts.	14.		
15. A net loss for the fiscal period is closed into the capital account by a debit to Revenue and Expense Summary and a credit to the capital account.	15.		
16. Balance sheet accounts normally have balances that carry over to succeeding fiscal periods.	16.		
17. A check stub should be completed before writing the check.	17.		
18. A bank statement balance will identify the checks that are outstanding.	18.		
19. Each petty cash voucher is the source document for a journal entry.	19.		
20. The petty cash fund replenishing entry results in debits to the various accounts for which petty cash was spent.	20.		

Part II Match the definition with the term by writing the appropriate *letter* in the column at the right. (A term is used once only.)

Terms

A. Accounts receivable
B. Asset
C. Balance
D. Bank statement
E. Closing entry
F. Creditor
G. Disbursement
H. Drawee
I. Endorsement in blank
J. Income statement
K. Journal
L. Ledger
M. Liabilities
N. Owner's equity
O. Payee
P. Post-closing trial balance
Q. Posting
R. Reconciliation statement
S. Restrictive endorsement
T. Revenue
U. Trial balance
V. Voucher

	Definitions		Letter
Example:	The value in an account		C
1.	A simple signature on the back of a check	1.	
2.	All accounts arranged by number	2.	
3.	Transferring entries from the journal to accounts	3.	
4.	A listing of all accounts with debit or credit balances for a work sheet	4.	
5.	The one to whom a debt is owed	5.	
6.	Payments made from the petty cash fund	6.	
7.	A statement prepared to find the correct checkbook and bank balance	7.	
8.	Income earned	8.	
9.	Any form used as a source document for a transaction	9.	
10.	A journal entry that zeros out an account balance	10.	
11.	Anything of value owned	11.	
12.	Net worth or capital	12.	
13.	Customers' accounts	13.	
14.	A chronological list of transactions, as a diary	14.	
15.	The bank on which a check is drawn	15.	

Part III For each of the following transactions, indicate the accounts to be debited and credited. Use the account titles listed at the left.

Account Titles	Transactions		Account Dr.	Account Cr.
	Example: Received $100 fee from customer.		A	G
A. Cash B. Supplies	1. Paid employee salary, $200.	1.		
C. Accounts Payable	2. Bought $30 worth of supplies for cash.	2.		
D. J. Owner, Capital	3. Invested $1,000 cash.	3.		
E. J. Owner, Drawing	4. Closed the revenue account.	4.		
F. Revenue and Expense Summary	5. Bought $500 worth of supplies, paying $100 down, and balance on account.	5.		
G. Commissions Income	6. Withdrew $150 cash for personal use.	6.		
H. Auto Expense I. Miscellaneous Expense	7. Closed the expense accounts	7.		
J. Salary Expense	8. Closed net income to owner's equity.	8.		
	9. Closed net loss to owner's equity.	9.		
	10. Closed the drawing account	10.		

Part IV (1) Complete Chet Gorski's work sheet.

(2) Complete a capital statement; assume that Gorski's capital includes a $5,000 investment during the year.

(3) Complete a balance sheet.

(4) Journalize the closing entries.

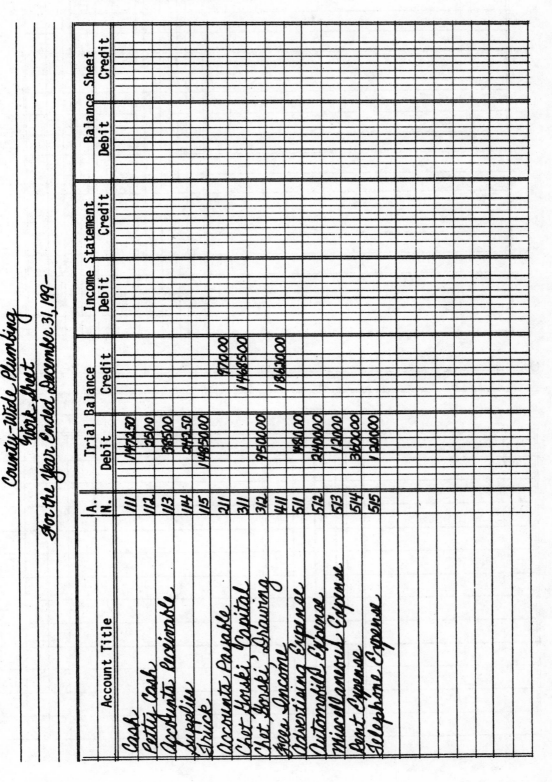

County-Wide Plumbing
Work Sheet
For the Year Ended December 31, 199–

Account Title	A. N.	Trial Balance Debit	Trial Balance Credit	Income Statement Debit	Income Statement Credit	Balance Sheet Debit	Balance Sheet Credit
Cash	111	1,472.50					
Petty Cash	112	25.00					
Accounts Receivable	113	385.00					
Supplies	114	242.50					
Truck	115	14,850.00					
Accounts Payable	211		970.00				
Chet Gorski, Capital	311		14,685.00				
Chet Gorski, Drawing	312	9,500.00					
Fees Income	411		18,620.00				
Advertising Expense	511	480.00					
Automobile Expense	512	2,400.00					
Miscellaneous Expense	513	120.00					
Rent Expense	514	3,600.00					
Telephone Expense	515	1,200.00					

(2)

(3)

(4) **GENERAL JOURNAL** Page 7

Part V (1) Complete the following check stub and check:

NO. 207	$ 35.50
DATE January 7	19 9-
TO Wilson Supply Co.	
FOR Smoke alarm (Equipment)	

	DOLLARS	CENTS
BAL. BRO'T FOR'D	382	47
AMT. DEPOSITED	225	00
TOTAL		
AMT. THIS CHECK		
BAL. CAR'D FOR'D		

No. ______

1-315
860

______ 19 ____

Pay to the order of ______ $ ______

______ Dollars

BOLTON NATIONAL BANK
of Long Island, NY

______

⑆0860⑉0830⑆ 1248⑉671⑈

(2) Record the journal entry for the above payment to Wilson Supply Company for the purchase of equipment.

CYCLE TWO
A Merchandising Business

WORDS TO REMEMBER

Controlling Account a *general ledger account* that shows the total balance of the individual *subsidiary* account balances, such as *accounts payable* and the separate *creditors' accounts*

Merchandise goods purchased to be sold to customers

Purchases Journal a special journal to record *only* the *purchases of merchandise on account* (payment to be made at a future date)

Schedule of Accounts Payable an end-of-the-month list of *all creditors* and the *amount owed to each*

CHAPTER 13 PURCHASES OF MERCHANDISE

Purchasing on Account—Accounts Payable

A merchandising business buys goods for resale to its customers; these goods are its MERCHANDISE. The usual procedure for most businesses is to buy ON ACCOUNT, rather than for cash. The balance is paid sometime in the future, perhaps within 30 to 60 days. As a result of such purchases, debts, called ACCOUNTS PAYABLE, are owed to creditors.

Purchases Journal

When many such purchases on account occur, it is preferred practice to record these transactions in a separate, special journal—a PURCHASES JOURNAL. This journal is used exclusively for recording one type of transaction—a *purchase of merchandise on account*.

This expense or *cost of merchandise* creates a new account, Purchases. Like expenses, *cost accounts increase by debits and decrease by credits*. If this entry appeared in *general journal* form, it would look as follows:

Date		Account	P.R.	Debit	Credit
199- Feb.	2	Purchases		500 00	
		Accounts Payable/B. Winslow	✓		500 00
		Purchases Invoice No. 152			

If there were many purchases of merchandise on account during a fiscal period, this entry would be repeated, and each entry would be posted to the Purchases account as well as the Accounts Payable account. (Purchases would be numbered 51; Accounts Payable would be numbered 21; all expenses would be renumbered, starting with 61.)

Posting Creditors' Accounts

To eliminate this repetitive posting to both Purchases and Accounts Payable, a PURCHASES JOURNAL is used. Creditors' accounts are posted for all entries so that up-to-date balances will be available. These accounts are located in a separate accounts payable ledger—a SUBSIDIARY LEDGER—where they are arranged alphabetically, or in some cases by special account number. Examine the following purchases journal entries:

PURCHASES JOURNAL Page 6

Date		From Whom Purchased - Account Credited	Invoice No.	PR	Purchases Dr. Accts. Pay. Cr.
199– apr.	2	Tri-Royal Sales Company	4834		3096 00
	7	Thomas Gregorius + Sons	045		375 00
	19	Vincent Morock, Inc.	380		400 00
	26	Thomas Gregorius + Sons	061		250 00

Each of these entries originated with a source document, an INVOICE, a statement or bill completed by the seller of merchandise. As can be seen from the following invoice, this form contains a complete description of the transaction. When received, it is checked against the merchandise that was shipped. Then it is recorded in the special purchases journal. Tri-Royal *sold* merchandise to Best-West and prepared the following invoice. Best-West *bought* merchandise from Tri-Royal and received a copy of that invoice, from which the purchases journal entry is made.

TRI-ROYAL SALES COMPANY
2158 Chambers Street
Trenton, NJ 08609

Sold to
Best-West Sewing Machine Corp
296 South Street
Newark, NJ 07114

Terms *30 days*

Invoice No. *4834*
Date *April 2, 199–*
Our Order No. *7985*
Customer's Order No. *924*
Shipped via *Truck*

Quantity	Description	Unit Price		Total Amount	
18	*EZ Sewing Machines #A15*	145	75	2623	50
75	*Hooks #H107*	6	30	472	50
				3096	00

Summarizing the Purchases Journal

The purchases journal is posted on a regular basis to creditors' accounts in the subsidiary ledger. At the end of the month, this journal is SUMMARIZED—totaled and ruled, and the total is posted to the accounts named in the column headed "Purchases Dr. and Accounts Payable Cr." These accounts are in the GENERAL LEDGER. In this way, the general ledger maintains debits equal to credits.

Review the purchases journal below, which has now been posted to both subsidiary and general ledger accounts. Note the 3-column arrangement of the creditors' accounts and the 4-column arrangement of the general ledger accounts. These provide for a balance *on the same line* as the entry — thus avoiding any pencil footings. To determine new balances, remember:

(1) Debit entries are added to prior debit balances.
(2) Credit entries are added to prior credit balances.
(3) Debit entries are deducted from prior credit balances.
(4) Credit entries are deducted from prior debit balances.

PURCHASES JOURNAL

Page 6

Date		From Whom Purchased - Account Credited		Invoice No.	PR	Purchases Dr. Accts. Pay. Cr.
199- Apr.	2	Tri-Royal Sales Company		4834	✓	3096 00
	7	Thomas Gregorius & Sons		045	✓	375 00
	19	Vincent Nurock, Inc.		380	✓	400 00
	26	Thomas Gregorius & Sons		061	✓	250 00
	30	Total				4121 00
						(51) (21)

ACCOUNTS PAYABLE LEDGER

Thomas Gregorius & Sons
515 Capital Avenue, Trenton, NJ 07114

Date			PR	Dr.	Cr.	Cr. Bal.
199- Apr.	7		P6		375 00	375 00
	26		P6		250 00	625 00

Vincent Nurock, Inc.
170 Underhill Boulevard, Syosset, NY 11791

Date			PR	Dr.	Cr.	Cr. Bal.
199- Mar.	4		P5		150 00	150 00
Apr.	19		P6		400 00	550 00

Tri-Royal Sales Company
2158 Chambers Street, Trenton, NJ 08609

Date			PR	Dr.	Cr.	Cr. Bal.
199- Feb.	28		P4		100 00	100 00
Mar.	18		P5		200 00	300 00
Apr.	2		P6		3096 00	3396 00

GENERAL LEDGER

Accounts Payable No. 21

Date			PR	Dr.	Cr.	Balance Dr.	Balance Cr.
199- Feb.	28		P4		100 00		100 00
Mar.	31		P5		350 00		450 00
Apr.	30		P6		4121 00		4571 00

Purchases No. 51

Date			PR	Dr.	Cr.	Balance Dr.	Balance Cr.
199- Apr.	30		P6	4121 00		4121 00	

The creditors' postings are indicated by check marks (√) in the purchases journal because these accounts have no numbers—they are arranged alphabetically. The journal total was posted to accounts No. 51 and No. 21 (Purchases and Accounts Payable).

In the accounts payable ledger, note carefully the three-column arrangement of creditors' accounts, some of which have balances carried over from prior months. A credit posting increases an account with a credit balance. We will see in Chapter 14 that posting debits to these accounts decreases their balances.

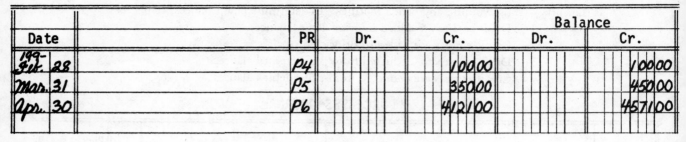

As stated above, posting references to creditors' accounts are indicated by check marks in the purchases journal because they have no account numbers. The journal total is posted to general ledger accounts and is indicated as accounts No. 51 and No. 21. This same technique for posting will be used whenever special journals are involved.

Schedule of Accounts Payable

At the end of the month, the accuracy of postings can be proved by preparing a SCHEDULE OF ACCOUNTS PAYABLE. This is a listing of creditors' accounts and the balance owed to each creditor. The total of the schedule should be equal to the balance in the CONTROLLING ACCOUNT—Accounts Payable—which shows in *total* balance the sum of the individual subsidiary account balances.

Best-West Sewing Machine Company
Schedule of Accounts Payable
April 30, 199-

Thomas Gregorius & Sons		625 00
Vincent Murock, Inc.		550 00
Tri-Royal Sales Company		3396 00
Total Accounts Payable		4571 00

YOU SHOULD REMEMBER

A purchases journal is a *book of original* entry, used only to record transactions for the *purchases of merchandise on account.*

The purchases journal *summary entry* posting is a *debit* to *Purchases* and a *credit* to *Accounts Payable.*

The schedule of accounts payable *total* equals the *balance* of the *Accounts Payable account.*

KNOW YOUR VOCABULARY

Accounts Payable	Purchases journal
Controlling account	Schedule of accounts payable
General ledger	Subsidiary ledger
Merchandise	Summarize (summary entry)
On account	

QUESTIONS

1. How does one distinguish between a service-type business and a merchandising business?
2. What type of transaction is recorded in a purchases journal?
3. How are creditors' accounts arranged in a subsidiary ledger?
4. How is the equality of general ledger debits and credits maintained when a special journal is used?
5. Why are creditors' accounts arranged alphabetically in a subsidiary ledger rather than numbered?
6. How is the accuracy of the subsidiary ledger proved?
7. What advantage is there in using a three-column ruling in creditors' accounts? A four-column ruling in general ledger accounts?

PROBLEMS

13–1 (1) Record the following purchases of merchandise on account on purchases journal page 5:

February 3, 199–	Dye & Akins, invoice No. 1705, $300
10,	Edward Kalpakian & Sons, invoice No. G-116, $425
17,	Dye & Akins, invoice No. 1751, $385
25,	Edward Kalpakian & Sons, invoice No. G-151, $500

(2) Post to the subsidiary ledger.

(3) Summarize the purchases journal at the end of the month, and post to the general ledger.

(4) Prepare a schedule of accounts payable for the owner, Ruth Ann Davis.

(1)

PURCHASES JOURNAL Page 2

(2)

Dye and Akins

199- Jan.	15		P1		450 00	450 00

Kalpakian & Sons

GENERAL JOURNAL

(3)

Accounts Payable No. 21

						Balance	
				Dr.	Cr.	Dr.	Cr.
199- Jan.	31		P1		450 00		450 00

Purchases No. 51

						Balance	
				Dr.	Cr.	Dr.	Cr.

(4)

13–2 (1) Record the following purchases of merchandise on account:

February 1, 199–	Paul Olins, invoice No. 42, $175
5,	Wilson & Shea, invoice No. 513, $200
8,	Island Supply, invoice No. 72A, $265
12,	Wilson & Shea, invoice No. 543, $400
15,	Glen Mfg., Inc., invoice No. 31, $620
19,	Paul Olins, invoice No. 78, $360
22,	Gregory Sims, invoice No. 318, $250
26,	Island Supply, invoice No. 29B, $300

(2) Post to the subsidiary ledger.

(3) Summarize the purchases journal at the end of the month, and post to the general ledger.

(4) Prepare a schedule of accounts payable for the owner, Paul Zagretti.

(1) PURCHASES JOURNAL Page 2

ACCOUNTS PAYABLE LEDGER

Glen Mfg., Inc.

(2)

Island Supply

Paul Olins

Gregory Sims

Wilson & Shea

(3) PURCHASES JOURNAL Page 2

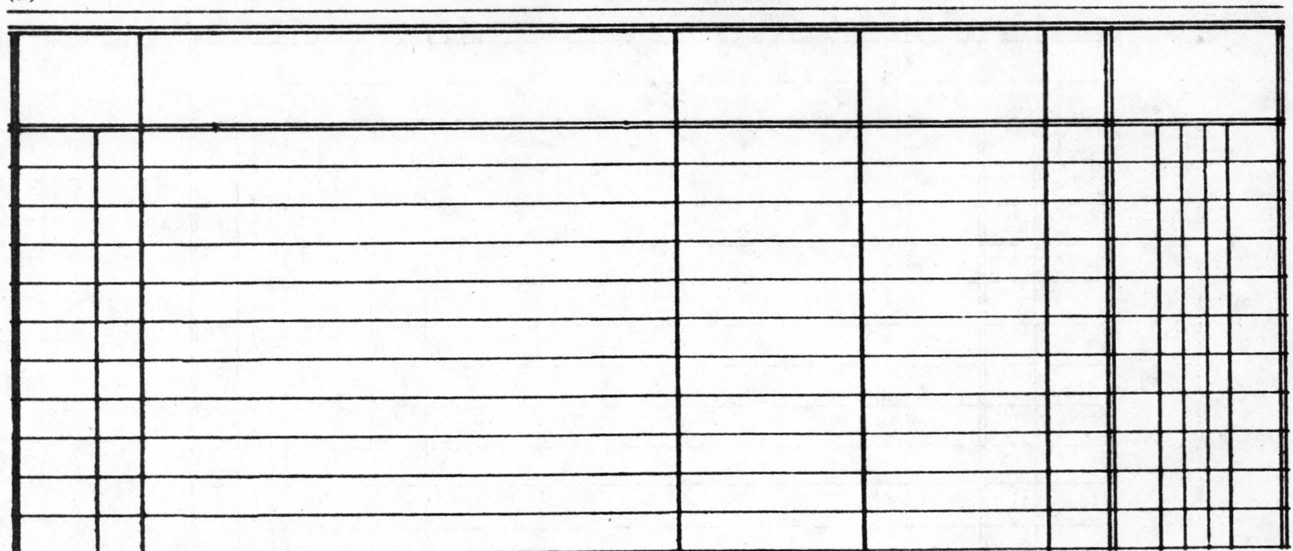

GENERAL LEDGER

Accounts Payable No. 21

				Dr.	Cr.	Balance Dr.	Balance Cr.

Purchases No. 51

				Dr.	Cr.	Balance Dr.	Balance Cr.

(4)

THINK IT OVER

By using a purchases journal, Harold Marino estimates that he saves at least one hour of posting time each week. How is this possible?

WORDS TO REMEMBER

Cash Disbursements Journal a special journal to record transactions *only for the payment of cash*

Special Columns account columns included in journals for *particular transactions* that occur often, thus *saving time in posting*

CHAPTER 14

CASH DISBURSEMENTS JOURNAL

A great number of business transactions involve the payment of cash, mostly by check. Such cash disbursements occur when invoices for merchandise purchased on account are paid, as well as payments for equipment, supplies, rent, salaries, and so on.

With each cash disbursement, a credit to cash must be recorded to decrease the Cash account. For each of these transactions, there also is a debit to the other account(s) involved. A typical *general journal* entry for a cash disbursement follows:

199- Mar.	2	Accounts Payable / John Reid Co.	✓	540 00	
		Cash			540 00
		Invoice No. 579, Check No. 318			

Columnar Journal —Special Columns

A general journal entry such as this requires postings to all accounts—Accounts Payable Debit, Cash Credit (in the general ledger), and John Reid Company's account debit (in the subsidiary ledger). It is preferable, therefore, to use a special CASH DISBURSEMENTS JOURNAL, which will require less frequent and fewer postings, and still keep creditors' accounts up to date. The entry shown above has been recorded in Jose Garcia's special journal, along with other typical cash disbursements transactions:

CASH DISBURSEMENTS JOURNAL — Page 1

Date		Account Debited	Ck. No.	PR	General Dr.	Accts. Pay. Dr.	Cash Cr.
199- Mar.	2	John Reid Company	318			54000	54000
	3	Rent Expense	319		30000		30000
	9	Supplies	320		7500		7500
	15	Salary Expense	321		15000		15000
	16	Union National Bank	322			40000	40000
	30	Jose Garcia, Drawing	323		50000		50000
	31	Los Angeles Distributing Co.	324			49500	49500

Note that there is a special column for the controlling account—Accounts Payable Dr. While postings are required for each account debited, *special column totals are posted only at the end of the month.* This journal is summarized, and the columns that have *identifiable account title headings* are posted as indicated—Accounts Payable Dr. (21) and Cash Cr. (11). The General Dr. column total is not posted and checked (√) because there is no *single* general ledger account for that total. Furthermore, the individual accounts listed as debited will have been posted.

Summarizing the Journal

Garcia's journal now appears as shown below, summarized and posted:

CASH DISBURSEMENTS JOURNAL — Page 1

Date		Account Debited	Ck. No.	PR	General Dr.	Accts. Pay. Dr.	Cash Cr.
199- Mar.	2	John Reid Company	318	√		54000	54000
	3	Rent Expense	319	54	30000		30000
	9	Supplies	320	14	7500		7500
	15	Salary Expense	321	55	15000		15000
	16	Union National Bank	322	√		40000	40000
	30	Jose Garcia, Drawing	323	32	50000		50000
	31	Los Angeles Distributing Co.	324	√		49500	49500
	31	Totals			102500	143500	246000
					(√)	(21)	(11)

First the columns were pencil footed; debit totals equal credit totals. Then they were written in ink, and the journal was double ruled. The General Dr. column total is always checkmarked, and the special column totals have been posted to the accounts identified in their headings. The postings to creditors' accounts and to the Cash and Accounts Payable accounts follow (General Dr. column account postings are not illustrated here):

GENERAL LEDGER

Cash — No. 11

				Dr.	Cr.	Balance Dr.	Balance Cr.
199– Mar.	31		CR	500000		500000	
	31		CD1		246000	254000	

Accounts Payable — No. 21

				Dr.	Cr.	Balance Dr.	Balance Cr.
199– Mar.	1	Balance	✓				54000
	31		P1		199500		253500
	31		CD1	143500			110000

ACCOUNTS PAYABLE LEDGER

Los Angeles Distributing Company
5001 Santa Monica Boulevard, Los Angeles, CA 90002

				Dr.	Cr.	Balance
199– Mar.	4		P1		49500	49500
	25		P1		100000	149500
	31		CD1	49500		100000

John Reed Company
72-05 Canyon Boulevard, Pasadena, CA 91100

				Dr.	Cr.	Balance
199– Mar.	1	Balance	✓			54000
	2		CD1	54000		

Union National Bank
452 Ocean Boulevard, San Diego, CA 92101

				Dr.	Cr.	Balance
199– Mar.	15		P1		50000	50000
	31		CD1	40000		10000

Schedule of Accounts Payable

At the end of the month, Jose Garcia's schedule of accounts payable is taken to prove the accuracy of the subsidiary ledger:

Jose Garcia
Schedule of Accounts Payable
March 31, 199-

Los Angeles Distributing Co.		1 000 00
Union National Bank		100 00
Total Accounts Payable		1 100 00

The balance of the controlling account, Accounts Payable, is also $1,100. The two are equal; the subsidiary ledger proves.

A cash disbursements journal may be expanded to include four or more columns, depending on the needs of the business. For example, if many *cash purchases* of merchandise occur, a special column—*Purchases Dr.*—can be included. Some businesses find it convenient to include a *Salary Expense Dr.* column as well. If these columns are included, it is necessary to checkmark (√) the posting reference column; no posting is needed for each cash purchases entry, inasmuch as *the column total will be posted*, along with all other special column totals, *at the end of the month.*

Examine these entries in a five-column cash disbursements journal:

CASH DISBURSEMENTS JOURNAL Page 4

		Account Debited	Ck. No.	PR	General Dr.	Accts. Pay. Dr.	Purchases Dr.	Salary Exp. Dr.	Cash Cr.
199- Mar.	4	Rent Expense	506		400 00				400 00
	7	Salary Expense	507	✓				250 00	250 00
	12	Purchases	508	✓			725 00		725 00
	19	Supplies Company	509			75 00			75 00
	26	Purchases	510	✓			300 00		300 00
	31	Totals			400 00	75 00	1 025 00	250 00	1 750 00
					(✓)	( )	( )	( )	( )

At the end of the month, the bookkeeping/accounting clerk can easily see which items need to be posted, and which do not. Those that are already checked *will not be posted*; items appearing in the *General Dr.* and *Accounts Payable Dr.* columns *will be posted* to the accounts identified in the account column. The *special column totals*—Accounts Payable Dr., Purchases Dr., Salary Expense Dr., and Cash Cr.—will be posted.

Source Document for Cash Disbursement

The cash disbursements journal, a multicolumn book of original entry, is used exclusively for entries that result in cash credits, which will cause a decrease in the amount of cash. For each entry, a check stub is identified as the source document in the Check Number (Ck. No.) column.

> **YOU SHOULD REMEMBER**
>
> Creditors' account balances should be kept up to date by frequent postings (daily or weekly).
>
> Special journal column *totals* are *posted* to the accounts identified *in the column heading.*

KNOW YOUR VOCABULARY

Cash disbursements journal   Summary entry

QUESTIONS

1. What advantage is there to using special journals for cash disbursements transactions, compared to using the general journal?
2. How are postings from a cash disbursements journal identified in the general ledger account?
3. What justifies the use of a special column in a cash disbursements journal?
4. How are postings to subsidiary ledger accounts indicated in the cash disbursements journal?
5. When does the check mark (√) indicate not to post?
6. When does the check mark indicate that the item has been posted?
7. How is the accuracy of the subsidiary ledger proved?

PROBLEMS

14–1 Sid Krasnoff uses a four-column cash disbursements journal with a special column for his personal cash withdrawals. Last month, his check stub record indicated the following:

March 1, Paid month's rent, $400; check No. 247
3, Paid utilities bill, $76.50; check No. 248
8, Paid Paula Cory on account, $50; check No. 249
10, Withdrew for personal use, $500; check No. 250
17, Paid employee's salary, $300; check No. 251
22, Paid Hilda Piper on account, $90; check No. 252
24, Withdrew for personal use, $500; check No. 253
29, Bought new equipment, $1,250; check No. 254
31, Paid employee's salary, $300; check No. 255

(1) Record each of these transactions, checking any entry that is not to be posted separately.

(2) Summarize the cash disbursements journal, checking any *total that is not to be posted.* Indicate by open parentheses ( ) totals that would be posted.

(1) and (2)

CASH DISBURSEMENTS JOURNAL Page 3

Date		Account Debited	Ck. No.	PR	General Dr.	Acct. Pay. Dr.	S. Krasnoff Draw. Dr.	Cash Cr.

14–2 Helen Scordas uses a special purchases journal and a three-column cash disbursements journal. Last month, she completed the following transactions:

April 1, Paid month's rent, $450; check No. 502
4, Purchased merchandise on account from Abel & Jenks, $600; invoice No. P-311
8, Withdrew for personal use $400; check No. 503
14, Paid Abel & Jenks on account $800; check No. 504
15, Paid employee's salary, $325; check No. 505
20, Purchased merchandise on account from W. T. Gross, $1,450; invoice No. 5113
22, Bought supplies, $75; check No. 506
28, Withdrew for personal use, $500; check No. 507
30, Paid W. T. Gross part on account, $725; check No. 508

(1) Record the entries for each transaction.
(2) Post the entries from the purchases journal.
(3) Post the entries from the cash disbursements journal.
(4) Summarize each journal, and post the column totals as indicated in the headings of each special column.
(5) Prove the accuracy of the subsidiary ledger by preparing a schedule of accounts payable.

(1) and (4)

PURCHASES JOURNAL Page 2

Date		Account Credited		Inv. No.	PR	Purchases Dr. Acct. Pay. Cr.

(1) and (4)

CASH DISBURSEMENTS JOURNAL

Page 3

Date		Acct. Dr.	Ck. No.	PR	General Dr.	Acct. Pay. Dr.	Cash Cr.

GENERAL LEDGER

Cash

No. 11

Date			PR	Dr.	Cr.	Balance Dr.	Balance Cr.
199- apr.	1	Balance	✓			4500 00	

Supplies

No. 13

Date			PR	Dr.	Cr.	Balance Dr.	Balance Cr.
199- apr.	1	Balance	✓			50 00	

(2) and (3)

Accounts Payable

No. 21

Date			PR	Dr.	Cr.	Balance Dr.	Balance Cr.
199- Apr.	1	Balance	✓				800 00

Helen Scordas, Drawing

No. 32

Date			PR	Dr.	Cr.	Balance Dr.	Balance Cr.

Purchases No. 51

Date			PR	Dr.	Cr.	Balance Dr.	Balance Cr.

Rent Expense No. 61

Date			PR	Dr.	Cr.	Balance Dr.	Balance Cr.

Salary Expense No. 62

Date			PR	Dr.	Cr.	Balance Dr.	Balance Cr.

ACCOUNTS PAYABLE LEDGER

(2) and (3)

Abel & Jenks
1200 Mineral Boulevard, Scranton, PA 18501

				Dr.	Cr.	Cr. Bal.
199- Apr.	1	Balance	✓			800 00

W. T. Gross
805 Keystone Road, Wilkes Barre, PA 18700

				Dr.	Cr.	Cr. Bal.

(5)

WORDS TO REMEMBER

Sales Journal a special journal to record transactions only for *the sale of merchandise on account*

Schedule of Accounts Receivable an end-of-month list of *all customers* and the *amount due from each*

CHAPTER 15 SALES OF MERCHANDISE

Sales on Account

For a merchandising business, the sale of merchandise is probably the most frequent of all transactions. In many large businesses, a major part of sales are ON ACCOUNT, that is, credit sales.

A general journal entry to record the sale of merchandise on account follows:

199– Apr.	7	Accounts Receivable/Alan Bergstrom	✓	175 00	
		Sales			175 00
		Sales Invoice No. 251			

Sales Journal and Accounts Receivable Ledger

If there were many sales similar to this one during a fiscal period, this entry would be repeated, and each entry would be posted to the Accounts Receivable account as well as to the Sales account. To eliminate the repetitive posting to both Accounts Receivable and Sales, a SALES

JOURNAL is used. Customers' accounts are posted for each entry so that up-to-date balances will be available. These accounts are located in another *separate subsidiary ledger*—an ACCOUNTS RECEIVABLE LEDGER—where accounts may be arranged alphabetically or, in some cases, by special account number. Examine the following sales journal entries:

SALES JOURNAL Page 8

Date		To Whom Sold - Account Debited	Invoice No.	PR	Accts. Rec. Dr. Sales Cr.
199- Apr.	2	Best-West Sewing Machine Company	4834		3096 00
	9	Elaine K. Brown	4835		175 00
	23	Ralph Mazel & Company	4836		250 00
	30	Elaine K. Brown	4837		200 00

Source Documents for Sales Journal Entries

Each of these entries originated with a source document, the invoice or sales slip, completed by the salesperson or the billing department of the seller. This invoice is prepared in TRIPLICATE copy; one copy is given to the customer, one copy is used by the shipping department, and one copy is sent to the accounting department for a source document to record the transaction. (Refer to the invoice on page 120: Tri-Royal Sales Company is the seller; Best-West Sewing Machine Company is the buyer, or the customer.)

Posting and Summarizing the Sales Journal

The sales journal is posted on a regular basis to customers' accounts in the subsidiary ledger. At the end of the month, this journal, like all special journals, is summarized, and the total is posted to the accounts named in the columns headed "Accounts Receivable Dr." and "Sales Cr." These accounts are in the general ledger, and by posting this total, debits will continue to equal credits.

Review the sales journal below, which has now been posted to both subsidiary and general ledger accounts:

SALES JOURNAL Page 8

Date		To Whom Sold - Account Debited	Invoice No.	PR	Accts. Rec. Dr. Sales Cr.
199- Apr.	2	Best-West Sewing Machine Company	4834	✓	3096 00
	9	Elaine K. Brown	4835	✓	175 00
	23	Ralph Mazel & Company	4836	✓	250 00
	30	Elaine K. Brown	4837	✓	200 00
	30	Total			3721 00
					(13) (41)

ACCOUNTS RECEIVABLE LEDGER

Best-West Sewing Machine Company
296 South Street, Newark, NJ 07114

Date			PR	Dr.	Cr.	Dr. Bal.
199- Apr.	1	Balance	✓			300 00
	2		S4	3096 00		3396 00

Elaine K. Brown
11 Harbor Road, Perth Amboy, NJ 08861

Date			PR	Dr.	Cr.	Dr. Bal.
199- Apr.	9		S4	175 00		175 00
	30		S4	200 00		375 00

Ralph Mazel & Company
278 Patriots Road, Morristown, NJ 07960

Date			PR	Dr.	Cr.	Dr. Bal.
199- Apr.	1	Balance	✓			400 00
	23		S4	250 00		650 00

GENERAL LEDGER

Accounts Receivable — No. 13

				Dr.	Cr.	Balance Dr.	Balance Cr.
199- Apr.	1	Balance	✓			700 00	
	30		S4	3721 00		4421 00	

Sales — No. 41

				Dr.	Cr.	Balance Dr.	Balance Cr.
199- Apr.	30		S4		3721 00		3721 00

The customers' postings are indicated by check marks (√) because these accounts have no numbers—they are arranged alphabetically. The journal total was posted to accounts No. 13 and No. 41 (Accounts Receivable and Sales).

The three-column subsidiary ledger arrangement is used also for customers' accounts. A debit increases the customer's account balance; a credit decreases the customer's account balance.

Schedule of Accounts Receivable

At the end of the month, the accuracy of postings can be proved by preparing a SCHEDULE OF ACCOUNTS RECEIVABLE. This is a listing of customers' accounts and the balance due from each. The total of the schedule should be equal to the balance of the controlling account—Accounts Receivable—which shows in *total* balance the sum of the individual subsidiary account balances.

Tri-Royal Sales Company
Schedule of Accounts Receivable
April 30, 199–

Best-West Sewing Machine Company		3396 00
Elaine K. Brown		375 00
Ralph Mazel & Company		650 00
Total Accounts Receivable		4421 00

YOU SHOULD REMEMBER

A sales journal is a book of *original* entry used only to record transactions for the *sale of merchandise on account.*

The sales journal *summary entry* posting is a *debit* to *Accounts Receivable* and a *credit* to *Sales.*

The schedule of Accounts Receivable *total* equals the *balance* of the *Accounts Receivable account.*

KNOW YOUR VOCABULARY

Accounts Receivable ledger

On account

Sales journal

Schedule of Accounts Receivable

Triplicate

QUESTIONS

1. What type of transaction is recorded in a sales journal?
2. How are customers' accounts arranged in a subsidiary ledger?
3. How is the equality of general ledger debits and credits maintained when posting a sales journal?

4. How is the accuracy of the subsidiary ledger proved?
5. Why might arranging customers' accounts alphabetically be easier for a small business to manage than numbering them?
6. Why are sales invoice numbers listed in consecutive order in a sales journal?

PROBLEMS

15–1 (1) Record Mear's Department Stores sales of merchandise on account, starting with invoice No. 215:

March 2, 199–	Mrs. Edward Ardyce, $175
9,	Mr. Herman Gold, $96.50
16,	Ms. Eliza Fisher, $107.30
23,	Mrs. Edward Ardyce, $62.45
30,	Ms. Eliza Fisher, $29.50

(2) Post to the subsidiary ledger.

(3) Summarize the sales journal at the end of the month, and post to the general ledger.

(4) Prepare a schedule of accounts receivable.

(1) and (3)

SALES JOURNAL

Page 31

Date		To Whom Sold - Account Debited	Invoice No.	PR	Acct. Rec. Dr. Sales Cr.

ACCOUNTS RECEIVABLE LEDGER

(2)

Mrs. Edward Ardyce
305 Riverview Terrace, Cincinnati, OH 45204

Date			PR	Dr.	Cr.	Dr. Bal.

Ms. Eliza Fisher
851 Clarkfield Street, Cincinnati, OH 45201

Date			PR	Dr.	Cr.	Dr. Bal.

Mr. Herman Gold
79 Willowbrook Drive, Cincinnati, OH 45202

Date			PR	Dr.	Cr.	Dr. Bal.
199- Mar	1	Balance	✓			258 60

GENERAL LEDGER

(3)

Accounts Receivable — No. 13

Date			PR	Dr.	Cr.	Balance Dr.	Balance Cr.
199- Mar	2	Balance	✓			258 60	

Sales — No. 41

				Dr.	Cr.	Balance Dr.	Balance Cr.

(4)

Mears Department Store
Schedule of Accounts Receivable
March 31, 199-

15–2 (1) Record the following sales of merchandise on account for Winslow's Emporium, starting with invoice No. 328:

April 2, 199–	Mrs. Fay Wilamowski, $47.50
6,	Ms. Shirley Callahan, $36.95
9,	Mr. William Witt, $49.25
13,	Ms. Shirley Callahan, $107.65
16,	Mrs. Marjorie Intrator, $76.80
20,	Mrs. Fay Wilamowski, $52.90
23,	Mr. William Witt, $59.20
27,	Mrs. Marjorie Intrator, $67.75
30,	Ms. Shirley Callahan, $87.00

(2) Post to the subsidiary ledger.

(3) Summarize the sales journal at the end of the month, and post to the general ledger.

(4) Prepare a schedule of accounts receivable.

(1) and (3)

SALES JOURNAL

Page 8

Date		To Whom Sold - Account Debited	Invoice No.	PR	Acct. Rec. Dr. Sales Cr.

ACCOUNTS RECEIVABLE LEDGER

(2)

Ms. Shirley Callahan
186 Mineola Boulevard, Mineola, NY 11501

Date			PR	Dr.	Cr.	Dr. Bal.
199- Apr.	1	Balance	✓			45 00

Mrs. Marjorie Intrator
91 Bryn Mawr, New Hyde Park, NY 11501

Date			PR	Dr.	Cr.	Dr. Bal.

Mrs. Fay Wilamowski
451 Cornell Drive, Hicksville, NY 11803

Date			PR	Dr.	Cr.	Dr. Bal.
199- Apr.	1	Balance	✓			65 30

Mr. William Witt
264 Emory Road, Mineola, NY 11501

Date			PR	Dr.	Cr.	Dr. Bal.
199- Apr.	1	Balance	✓			95 00

GENERAL LEDGER

(3) Accounts Receivable No. 13

Date		Item	P.R.	Dr.	Cr.	Balance Dr.	Balance Cr.
199- Apr.	1	Balance	✓			205 30	

Sales No. 41

Date		Item	P.R.	Dr.	Cr.	Balance Dr.	Balance Cr.

(4) Winslow's Emporium
Schedule of Accounts Receivable
April 30, 199-

THINK IT OVER

At last count, Lacy's Department Store had approximately 10,000 charge customers. Billing procedures are now fully automated, replacing hand operation. Exactly what has been accomplished (in bookkeeping terms) by the change?

Marshall & Kahn, a neighborhood specialty shop, is considering a change from a one-journal (general journal) bookkeeping/accounting system to using several special journals. What recommendations might be made to help in reaching a decision?

WORDS TO REMEMBER
Cash Receipts Journal a special journal to record transactions *only* for the *receipt of cash*
Detail Audit Tape a cumulative listing of all cash register transactions

CHAPTER 16

CASH RECEIPTS JOURNAL

Receiving cash from customers is another frequent transaction. Cash is received when a cash sale is made, or when it is received from a customer ON ACCOUNT for an outstanding balance due on a credit sale. Cash is also received when borrowed, whether from a bank or an individual. In each of these transactions, the cash is in the form of either currency or a check.

In each transaction, the result is an increase in the asset cash. Therefore, an entry must be made in which cash is debited. The corresponding credit indicates the source of the cash received. A typical *general journal* entry for a cash receipt follows:

199- Apr.	17	Cash		7500	
		Accounts Rec./Alan Bergstrom	✓		7500
		to Apply on Account			

Purpose of Cash Receipts Journal

General journal entries such as these require postings to all accounts—Cash Debit, Accounts Receivable Credit (in the general ledger), and Alan Bergstrom's account credit (in the subsidiary ledger). It is advisable, therefore, to use a special CASH RECEIPTS JOURNAL, which will involve less frequent and fewer postings and still keep customers' accounts up to date.

The same entry as shown above has been recorded in Betty Chan's special cash receipts journal, along with other typical cash receipts transactions:

CASH RECEIPTS JOURNAL Page 3

Date		Account Credited	PR	General Cr.	Accts. Rec. Cr.	Cash Dr.
199- Apr.	2	Gordon Robbins			50 00	50 00
	7	Betty Chan, Capital		2500 00		2500 00
	17	Alan Bergstrom			75 00	75 00
	19	Union National Bank		1000 00		1000 00
	25	Mabel Johnson			100 00	100 00
	30	Equipment		300 00		300 00

Posting to Accounts

Note that there is a special column for the controlling account—Accounts Receivable Cr. Postings are needed for all accounts credited, and are listed in the General Cr. and Accounts Receivable Cr. columns. Column totals, however, are *posted only at the end of the month*, when the journal is summarized. The columns that have identifiable account title headings are posted as indicated—Accounts Receivable Cr. (13) and Cash Dr. (11). The General Cr. column total is not posted and checked (√) because there is no *single* general ledger account for that total. Furthermore, the individual accounts listed as credited will have been posted.

Summarizing the Cash Receipts Journal

Betty Chan's journal now follows, posted and summarized:

CASH RECEIPTS JOURNAL Page 3

Date		Account Credited	PR	General Cr.	Accts. Rec. Cr.	Cash Dr.
199- Apr.	2	Gordon Robbins	√		50 00	50 00
	7	Betty Chan, Capital	31	2500 00		2500 00
	17	Alan Bergstrom	√		75 00	75 00
	19	Union National Bank	22	1000 00		1000 00
	25	Mabel Johnson	√		100 00	100 00
	30	Equipment	15	300 00		300 00
	30	Totals		3800 00	225 00	4025 00
				(√)	(13)	(11)

First, the columns were pencil footed; debit totals equal credit totals. Then they were written in ink, and the journal was double ruled. The General Dr. column is always checkmarked, and the special column totals have been posted to the accounts identified in their headings. The postings to customers' accounts and the Cash and Accounts Receivable accounts follow (General Cr. column account postings are not illustrated here):

GENERAL LEDGER

Cash No. 11

Date		Item	PR	Dr.	Cr.	Balance Dr.	Balance Cr.
199- Apr.	1	Balance	✓			78000	
	30		CR3	402500		480500	
	30		CD4		300000	180500	

Accounts Receivable No. 13

Date		Item	PR	Dr.	Cr.	Balance Dr.	Balance Cr.
199- Apr.	1	Balance	✓			30000	
	30		S5	120000		150000	
	30		CR3		22500	127500	

ACCOUNTS RECEIVABLE LEDGER

Alan Bergstrom
142 Overlook Drive, Minneapolis, MN 55402

Date			PR	Dr.	Cr.	Dr. Bal.
199- Apr.	7		S5	175 00		175 00
	17		CR3		75 00	100 00
	24		S5	500 00		600 00

Mabel Johnson
7103 River Road, St. Paul, MN 55101

Date			PR	Dr.	Cr.	Dr. Bal.
199- Apr.	1	Balance	✓			100 00
	15		S5	220 00		320 00
	25		CR3		100 00	220 00

Gordon Robbins
3216 Twin Oaks Avenue, Minneapolis, MN 55407

Date			PR	Dr.	Cr.	Dr. Bal.
199- Apr.	1	Balance	✓			200 00
	2		CR3		50 00	150 00
	22		S5	305 00		405 00

Schedule of Accounts Receivable

At the end of the month, Betty Chan's schedule of accounts receivable is taken to prove the accuracy of the subsidiary ledger:

Betty Chan Schedule of Accounts Receivable April 30, 199–		
Alan Bergstrom		600 00
Mabel Johnson		220 00
Gordon Robbins		455 00
Total Accounts Receivable		1 275 00

The balance of the controlling account, Accounts Receivable, is also $1,275. Since the balance in the controlling account equals the total of the subsidiary ledger, the accounts receivable ledger has been "proved."

Expanding the Journal

Any cash receipts journal may be expanded to include four or more columns, depending on the needs of the business. For example, if many *cash sales* of merchandise occur, a special column—Sales Cr.—can be included. If this column is used, it is necessary to checkmark (✓) the posting reference column; *no posting is needed for each cash sales entry,* inasmuch as the column total will be posted, along with all other *special column totals, at the end of the month.* Examine these entries in a four-column cash receipts journal:

Date		Account Debited	PR	General Cr.	Accts. Rec. Cr.	Sales Cr.	Cash Cr.
199– May	3	H.L. Wicker			100 00		100 00
	7	Sales	✓			500 00	500 00
	10	Mrs. D. Ginsburg			95 00		95 00
	14	Sales	✓			625 00	625 00
	17	Lawrence Evans, Cap.		4000 00			4000 00
	24	Sales	✓			595 00	595 00
	31	Sales	✓			850 00	850 00
	31	Totals		4000 00	195 00	2570 00	6765 00
				(✓)	( )	( )	( )

The bookkeeping/accounting clerk can easily see which items need to be posted, and which do not. Those that are checked *will not be posted*; items appearing in the *General Cr. and Accounts Receivable Cr. columns will be posted* periodically to the accounts identified in the Account Debited column. The *special column totals*—Accounts Receivable Cr., Sales Cr., and Cash Dr.—*will be posted* at the end of the month.

Source Documents for Cash Receipts

The cash receipts journal is a book of original entry, used exclusively for entries that result in cash debits—to increase the amount of cash. As with all entries, a source document is prepared for each cash receipt transaction; this may be a copy of a hand-prepared cash sales slip or a cash register DETAIL AUDIT TAPE, which accumulates a total of the cash register activity for each salesperson.

YOU SHOULD REMEMBER

Customers' account balances should be kept up to date by frequent (daily, weekly or monthly) posting.

Source documents are *business forms* that serve as *evidence of every transaction*, such as invoices (one copy is evidence of a sale on account, a duplicate copy is evidence of a purchase on account) and detail audit tapes.

KNOW YOUR VOCABULARY

Cash receipts journal — On account

Detail audit tape

QUESTIONS

1. What type of transaction is exclusively entered in a cash receipts journal?
2. What justifies the use of a special column in a cash receipts journal?
3. How are postings to subsidiary ledger accounts from the cash receipts journal indicated?
4. When does a check mark indicate a posting reference?
5. When does a check mark indicate that an item is not to be posted?
6. How is the accuracy of the accounts receivable ledger proved?

PROBLEMS

16–1 Raul Garcia, owner of the Rose of Texas Specialty Gift Shop, uses a four-column cash receipts journal. Subtotals are indicated in pencil for the first 3 weeks' entries.

(1) Continue by recording the following entries for the cash receipts transactions for the remainder of the month:

April 23, Garcia invested an additional $2,000 cash in his business
24, Borrowed $2,500 from Lone Star Bank; received a check for that amount
25, Received $85 from J. R. Dallas on account
26, Received $60 from Margo Chase on account
27, Sold old office typewriter (equipment) for $95 cash
28, Received $75 from Frances Lima on account
29, Cash sales for the week amounted to $1,765

(2) Summarize the journal at the end of the month. Checkmark all items *not to be posted* separately.

(3) Post the summary entry only.

(1) and (2)

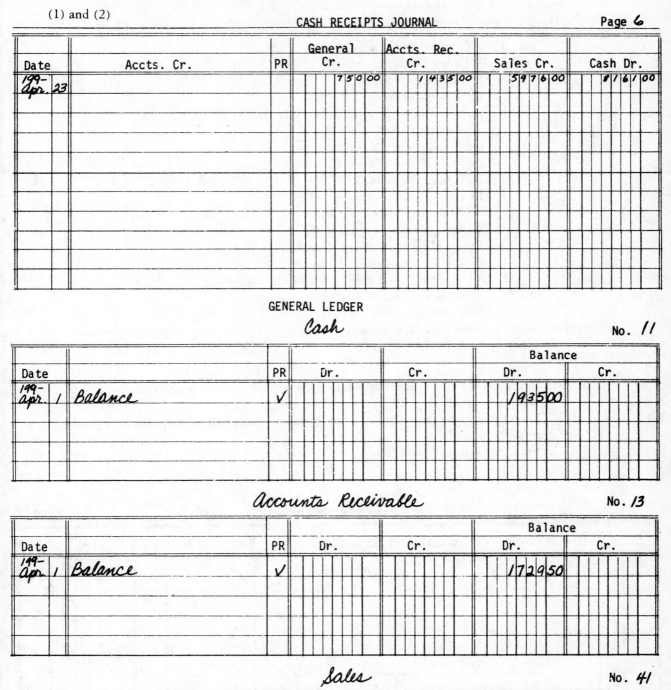

CASH RECEIPTS JOURNAL Page 6

Date		Accts. Cr.	PR	General Cr.	Accts. Rec. Cr.	Sales Cr.	Cash Dr.
199- Apr.	23			750 00	1 435 00	5 976 00	8 161 00

GENERAL LEDGER

Cash No. 11

Date			PR	Dr.	Cr.	Balance Dr.	Balance Cr.
199- Apr.	1	Balance	✓			1935 00	

Accounts Receivable No. 13

Date			PR	Dr.	Cr.	Balance Dr.	Balance Cr.
199- Apr.	1	Balance	✓			1729 50	

Sales No. 41

Date			PR	Dr.	Cr.	Balance Dr.	Balance Cr.
199- Mar.	31		S4		3500 00		3500 00
	31		CR5		6250 00		9750 00
	31		J3	9750 00			

16–2 Pat Norrell is a wholesaler who sells beauty shop supplies to barber shops and beauty salons. She uses a sales journal to record all sales of merchandise on account. She uses a four-column cash receipts journal with a sales credit column for cash sales made to customers to whom she sells merchandise for cash.

(1) Enter the following transactions for the month, starting with invoice No. 7156:

May 1,	Sold merchandise on account:
	Willow's Beauty Shoppe, $465
	Lee's Unisex, $395
7,	Cash sales for week, $252.50
10,	Received $200 from Goddess of Love
12,	Sold merchandise on account:
	Goddess of Love, $268.50
	Jayne's Curls & Waves, $175
14,	Cash sales for week, $307.25
15,	Invested an additional $3,000 cash
17,	Sold merchandise on account:
	Willow's Beauty Shoppe, $192
19,	Received $395 from Lee's Unisex
21,	Cash sales for week, $296.80
25,	Received $265 from Willow's Beauty Shoppe on account
28,	Cash sales for week, $319.90
29,	Sold merchandise on account:
	Jayne's Curls & Waves, $225
	Lee's Unisex, $315.20
31,	Cash sales for 3 days, $191.40

(2) Post current entries on a *weekly basis*, posting first the sales journal, then the cash receipts journal.

(3) Summarize the journals; post totals from the sales journal first, then the cash receipts journal.

(4) Prepare a schedule of accounts receivable.

(1)

SALES JOURNAL

Page 9

Date		To Whom Sold - Account Debited	Invoice No.	PR	Acct. Rec. Dr. Sales Cr.

CASH RECEIPTS JOURNAL

Page 6

Date		Account Credited	PR	General Cr.	Accts. Rec. Cr.	Sales Cr.	Cash Dr.

(2) and (3)

ACCOUNTS RECEIVABLE LEDGER

Goddess of Love
110 Chemung Avenue, Binghamton, NY 13901

Date		PR	Dr.	Cr.	Dr. Bal.
199- May 1	Balance	✓			200 00

Jayne's Curls & Waves
39 Tompkins Avenue, Cortland, NY 13045

Date		PR	Dr.	Cr.	Dr. Bal.

Lee's Unisex
451 College Heights Road, Ithaca, NY 14850

Date		PR	Dr.	Cr.	Dr. Bal.

Willow's Beauty Shoppe
58 Twain Boulevard, Elmira, NY 14901

Date		PR	Dr.	Cr.	Dr. Bal.

GENERAL LEDGER

(3)

Cash — Page 11

Date			PR	Dr.	Cr.	Balance Dr.	Balance Cr.
199- May	1	Balance	✓			1078 50	

Accounts Receivable — No. 13

Date			PR	Dr.	Cr.	Balance Dr.	Balance Cr.
199- May	1	Balance	✓			200 00	

Pat Norrell, Capital — No. 31

Date			PR	Dr.	Cr.	Balance Dr.	Balance Cr.
199- May	1	Balance	✓				25000 00

Sales — No. 41

Date			PR	Dr.	Cr.	Balance Dr.	Balance Cr.

(4)

WORDS TO REMEMBER

Correcting Entry an entry to correct an error (usually a posting error) made *during an earlier fiscal period*

Memorandum a business form used to record a *reduction in the amount owed* (*or due*) because of the *return and/or allowance* granted *by the seller to the buyer* of goods or services

Statement of Account a bill *sent by the seller* to each charge customer that summarizes that month's transactions and indicates any balance due

GENERAL JOURNAL, FOUR-COLUMN FORMAT

There are several reasons why customers may return merchandise that was sold to them. It may be damaged, the wrong size, the wrong color, or otherwise unsatisfactory. In other cases, customers may retain possession of the merchandise but receive a reduction in the selling price.

Sales Returns and Allowances, and Purchases Returns and Allowances

In either case, a new account is involved in each of these transactions—either SALES RETURNS AND ALLOWANCES or PURCHASES RETURNS AND ALLOWANCES. A *general journal* entry illustrating the first of these follows:

Date		Account	P.R.		Debit		Credit
199– May	23	Sales Returns and Allowances	411		25 75		
		Accts Receivable / J. Falkin	113/✓				25 75
		Credit Memo No. 135					

Posting references are given to show how this is handled. Because Sales Returns and Allowances represent decreases in Sales, the special numbering sequence for such VALUATION ACCOUNTS is indicated by the use of a decimal figure, as account No. 41.1. (Purchases Returns and Allowances would be account No. 51.1, which indicates decreases in Purchases.) Accounts Receivable was posted to account No. 13, and Judith Falkin was posted (✓) to a subsidiary ledger account.

Source Documents

The source document for such an entry is a CREDIT MEMORANDUM, a form that is similar in appearance to the original invoice but has the words "Credit Memorandum" printed at the top and is often printed on pink paper. A copy is given to the customer (the buyer) who returns merchandise and/or is being given an allowance (by the seller).

Note the use of the diagonal line in the Posting Reference column for the credit part of this entry. Both accounts are posted—one to a general ledger account, and one to a subsidiary ledger account.

Examine carefully how the same entry is recorded in a *four-column general journal*, using columns for controlling accounts: Accts. Pay. Dr. and Accts. Rec. Cr.

GENERAL JOURNAL

Page

Accts. Pay. Dr.	General Dr.	Date		PR	General Cr.	Accts. Rec. Cr.
	25 75	199- May 23	Sales Returns and Allowances	41.1		
			Judith Falkin	✓		25 75
			Credit Memo No. 135			

Only two postings are needed for this entry—Sales Returns and Allowances and Judith Falkin. At the end of the month, the journal is summarized. The totals for the General Dr. and General Cr. columns are checkmarked, and the special columns are posted to the accounts indicated in their headings. Compare this to the entry on page 159.

A four-column general journal with typical entries follows. Explanations are given below the journal.

GENERAL JOURNAL Page 4

Accts. Pay. Dr.	General Dr.	Date		PR	General Cr.	Accts. Rec. Cr.
	50 00	199- May 2	Priscilla Deutsch			
			Priscilla Deitch		50 00	
			Correct Posting Error 4/18/8-			
	260 00	9	Martin Hande, Drawing			
			Purchases		260 00	
			Merchandise for Personal Use			
	25 75	23	Sales Returns and Allowances			
			Judith Falkin			25 75
			Credit Memo No. 135			
75 00		25	Kevin Sullivan & Company			
			Purchases Returns and		75 00	
			Allowances			
			Debit Memo No. 52			
	275 00	29	Equipment			
			Martin Hande, Capital		275 00	
			Transferred Typewriter to			
			Business			
75 00	610 75	31	Totals		660 00	25 75
( )	(✓)				(✓)	( )

Correcting Errors in Ledger Postings

On May 2, a CORRECTING ENTRY was made. Because of similarity in names, a posting error was made last month. A charge to Priscilla Deutsch for merchandise sold on account was posted to Priscilla Deitch. It appears as a debit in the wrong account. It should be in the Deutsch account. This entry corrects the error and can be entered in the General Dr. and General Cr. columns, inasmuch as it *does not affect* the Accounts Receivable account.

On May 9, the owner, Martin Hande, withdrew *merchandise* for personal use. Merchandise *purchased* for resale to customers is, therefore, reduced by the cost price of whatever was withdrawn. Since purchases are debits, *withdrawals of merchandise are credits to the Purchases account.*

On May 23, a charge customer, Judith Falkin, returned damaged merchandise for credit. Credit memorandum No. 135 was completed, and a copy (source document) used for this entry, which *decreases the customer's account balance.* Since this amount is entered in the controlling account column, it will also decrease that account balance when the column total is posted at the end of the month.

On May 25, the owner returned merchandise purchased on account to a creditor, Kevin Sullivan & Company. This is a DEBIT MEMORANDUM, a copy of the original memorandum completed by the seller. This entry *decreases the balance owed to the creditor*, as well as the controlling account when the column total is posted at the end of the month.

On May 29, the owner transferred to his business a typewriter formerly used at home. This increases his owner's equity, as any investment would.

At the end of the month, the general journal summary entry shows that the General Dr. and General Cr. column totals are checkmarked. They are not to be posted. The individual items in these two columns will be posted daily (or as soon as possible) during the month. The special account column totals will be posted to accounts identified in their headings. In this way, the controlling accounts—Accounts Receivable and Accounts Payable—will continue to show in totals what individual customers' and creditors' accounts show in their respective subsidiary ledgers.

Statement of Account

Periodically—at the end of each month, or at set dates during the month—the seller of merchandise sends each charge customer a STATEMENT OF ACCOUNT. This "bill" may be in the form of punched cards or of a detailed list of all transactions. Illustrated below is a statement sent by a seller to one of its charge customers:

BOSTON WHOLESALE SUPPLY COMPANY
1219 Beacon Street
Boston, MA 02105

May 31 19 9-

Mr. James Wolff
351 Tremont Street
Brighton, MA 02135

		CHARGES		
May 4	19-	Sales Slip No. 408	25 00	
22	19-	Sales Slip No. 573	40 00	65 00
		PAYMENTS/RETURNS		
May 28	19-	Check No. 79	25 00	
28	19-	Credit Memo No. 91	15 00	40 00
		Balance Due		25 00

The charges are debit postings to this customer's account. The payment/returns are credit postings. The balance due is the same as the last balance in the customer's account. Occasionally a *customer may overpay* an account (the balance due). Should this happen, there would be a *credit balance* in the customer's account, an account that normally has a debit balance. (If a creditor's account is overpaid, there would be a *debit balance* in an account that normally has a credit balance.)

A *cash refund or allowance* may be given to a *customer*. This is a cash disbursements journal entry in which Sales Returns and Allowances is debited and Cash is credited. If the *buyer* is given the cash refund or allowance, a cash receipts journal entry will be made in which Purchases Returns and Allowances is credited and Cash is debited.

YOU SHOULD REMEMBER

A four-column general journal includes special columns for any *debits* to *Accounts Payable* and any *credits* to *Accounts Receivable.*

General debit and credit *column totals* are *checkmarked* to indicate that those *totals are not to be posted.*

Valuation accounts (returns and allowance accounts) *reduce* the balance of the account to which they are "related."

KNOW YOUR VOCABULARY

- Correcting entry
- Credit memorandum
- Debit memorandum
- Purchases returns and allowances
- Sales returns and allowances
- Statement of account
- Valuation account

QUESTIONS

1. What are the column headings of a four-column general journal?
2. What is the posting procedure from a four-column general journal?
3. What kinds of entries are recorded in a general journal?
4. Henry Jones sold merchandise to Claire Smith on account. Part of it is returned for credit. What entry is made in Jones's records? What entry is made in Smith's records?
5. What is the source document for Jones's entry? What is the source document for Smith's entry?
6. What information is reported in a customer's statement of account?

PROBLEMS

17–1 (1) Record the following entries on journal page 7 for Philip Scheiber, the owner of Scheiber's Music Emporium:

May 2, Allowed Jane McDonald $35 credit for damaged merchandise; credit memo No. 18

5, Correct $65 posting error for sale on account to Hedy Nachtigal, posted incorrectly to Netty Nachtigal

9, Received $100 allowance on merchandise purchased from Baldwin Piano Company; debit memo No. 53

15, Took a $95 guitar as a gift for nephew

22, Allowed Alice Glaser $80 credit for return of damaged merchandise; credit memo No. 19

29, Transferred a $185 desk from home to the business office

(2) Summarize the general journal and indicate by a check mark any column total *not to be posted.*

(1) and (2)

GENERAL JOURNAL

Page 7

Accts. Pay. Dr.	General Dr.	Date		PR	General Cr.	Accts. Rec. Cr.

17–2 Record the following entries on journal page 5 for Carol Dambroff, owner of Carol's Quality Draperies:

May 3, Returned to Home Decorator's Corp. $160 worth of poor quality merchandise purchased on account last month; debit memo No. AR-51

10, Paid $38 cash refund to customer who returned merchandise; check No. 326

17, Granted a $77 credit to Mrs. Robin Muir for merchandise returned; credit memo No. 39

24, Received a $50 cash refund for wrong-size merchandise paid for last month

28, Correct $140 posting error for purchase on account from C. Wilton Fabric Company, credited incorrectly to Carl Walton Furniture Company's account

GENERAL JOURNAL

Page 5

Accts. Pay Dr.	General Dr.	Date		PR	General Cr.	Accts. Rec. Cr.

CASH RECEIPTS JOURNAL

Page 12

Date	Acct. Cr.	PR	Gen. Cr.	Acct. Rec. Cr.	Sales Cr.	Cash Dr.

CASH DISBURSEMENTS JOURNAL

Page 11

Date	Acct. Dr.	Ck. No.	PR	Gen. Dr.	Acct. Pay. Dr.	Purch. Dr.	Cash Cr.

17–3 Below is the ledger account for a customer, Pearl Nathanson, of Hudson's Department Store. Prepare a statement of account, dated May 20.

Ms. Pearl Nathanson
972 Riverside Dr.
St. Louis, MO 63104

Date			Ref.	Debit	Credit	Balance
199- May	1		S3	60 00		60 00
	5		S4	75 00		135 00
	12		J2		35 00	100 00
	15		CR5		20 00	75 00
	18		S5	45 00		120 00

STATEMENT OF ACCOUNT

Hudson's Department Store
100 Gateway Plaza
St. Louis, MO 63101

SOLD TO

______________________ ______________ 19____

		CHARGES		
		PAYMENTS/CREDITS		

17–4 Comprehensive Five-Journal Problem.

Edward Shaw owns and operates a retail jewelry business. He uses special journals for

(1) sales of merchandise on account,
(2) purchases of merchandise on account,
(3) cash disbursements,
(4) cash receipts, and
(5) all other transactions are recorded in a general journal.

(1) Record the following transactions in the appropriate journals:

May 1, 199–	Paid Winslow Jewelers $465; check No. 392
	Paid rent for month $450; check No. 393
3,	Received cash on account from:
	Marc Green, $150
	Gian Polidoro, $95
4,	Sold merchandise on account to:
	Antonio Lorenzo, $300; invoice No. B192
	Edward Grabczak, $250; invoice No. B193
8,	Correct $35 posting error for supplies incorrectly posted to Equipment
11,	Sold merchandise on account to Marc Green, $275; invoice No. B194
13,	Withdrew $500 *cash* for personal use; check No. 394
14,	Paid clerks' salaries, $300; check No. 395
17,	Purchased merchandise on account:
	Schmidt & Brendle, $375
	Winston Jewelers, $1,200
22,	Received cash on account from:
	Antonio Lorenzo, $50
	Edward Grabczak, $125
24,	Allowed $75 credit to Marc Green for damaged merchandise; credit memo No. 35
28,	Paid Schmidt & Brendle $375; check No. 396
29,	Paid $40 refund to customer for returned merchandise; check No. 397
31,	Cash sales to date, $2,740
31,	Took a $200 ring home as gift for wife

(2) Summarize all journals. Checkmark any items, current entries and totals, that are not to be posted.

PURCHASES JOURNAL Page 10

Date		Account Credited		Inv. No.	PR	Purchases Dr. Acct. Pay. Cr.

SALES JOURNAL

Page 14

Date		Account Debited	PR	Acct. Rec. Dr Sales Cr.

CASH RECEIPTS JOURNAL

Page 19

Date			PR	Gen. Cr.	Acct. Rec. Cr	Sales Cr.	Cash Dr.
199- May	1	Balance on hand $1,500	✓				

CASH DISBURSEMENTS JOURNAL Page 17

Date		Ck. No.	PR	Gen. Dr.	Acct. Pay. Dr.	Purch. Dr.	Cash Cr.

GENERAL JOURNAL Page 5

Acct. Pay. Dr.	Gen. Dr.	Date		PR	Gen. Cr.	Acct. Rec. Cr.

WORDS TO REMEMBER

Adjusting Entry an entry made at the *end of a fiscal period* to bring *an account balance up to date*
Partnership a *business organization* that is *owned by two or more* persons, who operate it by mutual agreement
Prepaid Expenses *assets that become expenses* by being used up within a short period of time

CHAPTER 18 EIGHT-COLUMN WORK SHEET

Up to this point in a merchandising business, the bookkeeping/accounting cycle has followed these steps:

(1) A business transaction occurs, resulting in a source document—an invoice (sales and purchases), a check, a debit or credit memorandum, and so on.
(2) The transaction is journalized.
(3) The journal entry is posted to ledger accounts; summary entries are posted.

Trial Balance

To complete all the work required in the cycle, a trial balance is prepared. This may be a separate, formal statement, or it may be completed as the first two columns of an EIGHT-COLUMN WORK SHEET. This trial balance is a listing of *all general ledger accounts*, including those that do not have balances—Revenue and Expense Summary, and certain expenses as well.

Adjusting Entries

An eight-column work sheet provides columnar space to adjust the accounts that have not been kept up to date. Some changes in account balances were not recorded in the journals, and therefore not posted to accounts. It is now necessary to bring them up to date. This is accomplished by entering ADJUSTMENTS in the special work sheet columns.

MERCHANDISE INVENTORY

In a merchandising business, one of the major assets is the MERCHANDISE INVENTORY. As merchandise is purchased and sold, however, no entries are made to the Merchandise Inventory account. All purchases are debits to the Purchases account; all sales are credits to the Sales account. However, the cost value (or possibly some other basis for evaluating merchandise) is an asset value. At the end of each fiscal period, the new, closing, or ending inventory is taken. The beginning, or opening, inventory (last fiscal period's ending inventory) has undoubtedly been sold, and is, therefore, part of the revenue and expense for the fiscal period. To record this change in inventory values, adjusting entries are made on the work sheet. See adjusting entry (A) in the sample work sheet on page 173, which *debits Revenue and Expense Summary* and *credits Merchandise Inventory*, using the amount of the *old, beginning inventory*. This actually "zeroes out" the Merchandise account balance. To record the new, ending inventory, adjusting entry (B) *debits Merchandise Inventory* and *credits Revenue and Expense Summary*, using the amount of the inventory at the *end of the fiscal period.*

SUPPLIES

The trial balance lists the SUPPLIES account at its beginning balance, plus any supplies acquired during the fiscal period. The fact that some of these supplies may have been used during the fiscal period has not been recorded. Therefore a supplies inventory is taken to determine the value on hand at the end of the fiscal period. To find the *amount used* during that time, the ending inventory is subtracted from the account balance. The *difference is the expense* for supplies. See adjusting entry (C), which *debits Supplies Expense* and *credits Supplies* for that *difference.*

OTHER PREPAID EXPENSES

Other PREPAID EXPENSES—assets such as prepaid insurance, which become expenses by being used up in a relatively short period—are adjusted in the same way. Their respective expense accounts are debited, and the prepaid assets are credited for *the amount used* during the fiscal period.

Extending Updated Balances

Each of the amounts is extended to one of the remaining columns to complete the work sheet. Examine each account, its debits and/or credits, in the first four columns, in order to determine the updated balance or amount to be extended to one of the remaining four columns in either the Income Statement or the Balance Sheet column. Revenue and Expense Summary adjustment figures are carried to *both* Income Statement columns; each of the other account balances is extended to only one column.

Determining Net Income or Net Loss

When the extensions are completed properly, the *differences between the total debits and credits in the Income Statement columns and the total debits and credits in the Balance Sheet columns should be equal.* The amount is either a net income or a net loss for the fiscal period—*net income* if the Income Statement credit column total is greater than the debit column; *net loss* if the reverse is true.

The amount of net income is entered in each pair of columns, to be added to the smaller column total, thus giving two equal totals for each pair of columns. In the Income Statement columns, the total is entered in the debit column; in the Balance Sheet columns, it is entered in the credit column. The final equal totals are then double ruled, and the words "Net Income" are written on the proper line in the Account Title column.

Fields and Ross
Work Sheet
For Year Ended December 31, 199-

Account Title	A. N.	Trial Balance Debit	Trial Balance Credit	Adjustments Debit	Adjustments Credit	Income Statement Debit	Income Statement Credit	Balance Sheet Debit	Balance Sheet Credit
Cash	111	2250 00						2250 00	
Petty Cash	112	50 00						50 00	
Accounts Receivable	113	3175 00						3175 00	
Merchandise Inventory	114	15500 00		(B) 13600 00	(A) 15500 00			13600 00	
Equipment	115	15000 00						15000 00	
Supplies	116	1390 00			(C) 950 00			440 00	
Accounts Payable	211		2050 00						2050 00
A. G. Fields, Capital	311		11595 00						11595 00
A. G. Fields, Drawing	311.1	12000 00						12000 00	
B. W. Ross, Capital	312		12610 00						12610 00
B. W. Ross, Drawing	312.1	12000 00						12000 00	
Revenue and Expense Summary	313			(A) 15500 00	(B) 13600 00	15500 00	13600 00		
Sales	411		76000 00				76000 00		
Sales Returns + Allow.	411.1	1750 00				1750 00			
Purchases	511	30000 00				30000 00			
Purchases Returns + Allow.	511.1		580 00				580 00		
Advertising Expense	611	1200 00				1200 00			
Miscellaneous Expense	612	120 00				120 00			
Rent Expense	613	2400 00				2400 00			
Salary Expense	614	6000 00				6000 00			
Supplies Expense	615			(C) 950 00		950 00			
		102835 00	102835 00	30050 00	30050 00	57920 00	90180 00	58515 00	26255 00
Net Income						32260 00			32260 00
						90180 00	90180 00	58515 00	58515 00

Notice that the completed work sheet on page 173 is for a PARTNERSHIP, Fields and Ross. In a partnership, two or more individuals combine their investments and operate a business according to an agreement. The amounts invested, the responsibilities of the partners, and the method for sharing net income or net losses should be spelled out in detail. In that way future disagreements may be avoided.

YOU SHOULD REMEMBER

The Revenue and Expense Summary account is used to *make certain adjusting entries* (for merchandise inventory) at the end of a fiscal period.

Prepaid expenses *are assets when first acquired*, but become expenses as they are used, thus requiring an adjustment to record this change.

KNOW YOUR VOCABULARY

Adjustments (adjusting entries)

Eight-column work sheet

Merchandise inventory

Partnership

Prepaid assets

QUESTIONS

1. What are the four headings for the four pairs of columns in an eight-column work sheet?
2. How is the end-of-fiscal-period merchandise inventory determined?
3. What does the first merchandise adjusting entry (A) accomplish?
4. What does the second merchandise adjusting entry (B) accomplish?
5. How are the Balance Sheet column extended amounts determined for
   a) merchandise inventory, and
   b) prepaid expenses?
6. Why do prepaid expenses have to be adjusted at the end of a fiscal period?
7. How is a net income for the fiscal period determined?
8. How is a net loss for the fiscal period determined?

PROBLEMS

(Save your work for use in Chapters 19 and 20.)

18–1 Daniel Green's general ledger account balances are given below:

Cash	$ 1,200
Accounts Receivable	2,500
Merchandise Inventory	5,000
Equipment	6,000
Supplies	400
Accounts Payable	1,800
Daniel Green, Capital	14,200
Daniel Green, Drawing	1,500
Revenue and Expense Summary	---
Sales	6,500
Sales Returns and Allowances	250
Purchases	3,000
Purchase Returns and Allowances	150
Miscellaneous Expense	100
Rent Expense	1,200
Salary Expense	1,500
Supplies Expense	---

Complete the work sheet on page 176 for the quarter ended June 30, 199–, using the following information for adjustments:

Merchandise inventory, June 30	$5,175
Supplies on hand	$ 300

18–2 Timothy Sullivan's general ledger is given on pages 177–180. Complete the eight-column work sheet on page 181, using the following additional information:

Merchandise Inventory, Jan. 31	$3,950
Supplies on hand	$ 205
Prepaid insurance	$ 250

Account Title	A. N.	Trial Balance		Adjustments		Income Statement		Balance Sheet	
		Debit	Credit	Debit	Credit	Debit	Credit	Debit	Credit

Cash No. 11

Date			PR	Dr.	Cr.	Balance Dr.	Balance Cr.
199- Jan	1	Balance	✓			1500 00	
	31		CR2	3650 00		5150 00	
	31		CP3		1790 00	3360 00	

Accounts Receivable No. 12

Date			PR	Dr.	Cr.	Balance Dr.	Balance Cr.
199- Jan.	1	Balance	✓			500 00	
	31		S2	3200 00		3700 00	
	31		CR2		150 00	3550 00	
	31		J1		35 00	3515 00	

Merchandise Inventory No. 13

Date			PR	Dr.	Cr.	Balance Dr.	Balance Cr.
199- Jan.	1	Balance	✓			3800 00	

Supplies No. 14

Date			PR	Dr.	Cr.	Balance Dr.	Balance Cr.
199- Jan.	1	Balance	✓			275 00	
	3		CP2	50 00		325 00	

Prepaid Insurance No. 15

Date			PR	Dr.	Cr.	Balance Dr.	Balance Cr.
199- Jan	1	Balance	✓			30000	

Accounts Payable No. 21

Date			PR	Dr.	Cr.	Balance Dr.	Balance Cr.
199- Jan.	1	Balance	✓				100000
	31		P2		120000		220000
	31		CP3	40000			180000

Timothy Sullivan, Capital No 31

Date			PR	Dr.	Cr.	Balance Dr.	Balance Cr.
199- Jan	1	Balance	✓				537500
	10		CR3		250000		787500

Timothy Sullivan, Drawing No 32

Date			PR	Dr.	Cr.	Balance Dr.	Balance Cr.
199- Jan	15		CP2	15000		15000	
	30		CP2	15000		30000	

Revenue and Expense Summary No. 33

Date			PR	Dr.	Cr.	Balance Dr.	Balance Cr.

Sales No. 41

Date			PR	Dr.	Cr.	Balance Dr.	Balance Cr.
199- Jan	31		S2		3200 00		3200 00
	31		CR2		1000 00		4200 00

Sales Returns and Allowances No. 41.1

Date			PR	Dr.	Cr.	Balance Dr.	Balance Cr.
199- Jan	20		J2	35 00		35 00	

Purchases No. 51

Date			PR	Dr.	Cr.	Balance Dr.	Balance Cr.
199- Jan	31		P2	1200 00		1200 00	
	31		CP3	500 00		1700 00	

Advertising Expense — No. 61

Date			PR	Dr.	Cr.	Balance Dr.	Balance Cr.
199-							
Jan	3		CP2	100 00		100 00	

Insurance Expense — No. 62

Date			PR	Dr.	Cr.	Balance Dr.	Balance Cr.

Miscellaneous Expense — No. 63

Date			PR	Dr.	Cr.	Balance Dr.	Balance Cr.
199-							
Jan	12		CP2	25 00		25 00	
	27		CP2	15 00		40 00	

Rent Expense — No. 64

Date			PR	Dr.	Cr.	Balance Dr.	Balance Cr.
199-							
Jan	2		CP2	400 00		400 00	

Supplies Expense — No. 65

Date			PR	Dr.	Cr.	Balance Dr.	Balance Cr.

Account Title	A. N.	Trial Balance		Adjustments		Income Statement		Balance Sheet	
		Debit	Credit	Debit	Credit	Debit	Credit	Debit	Credit

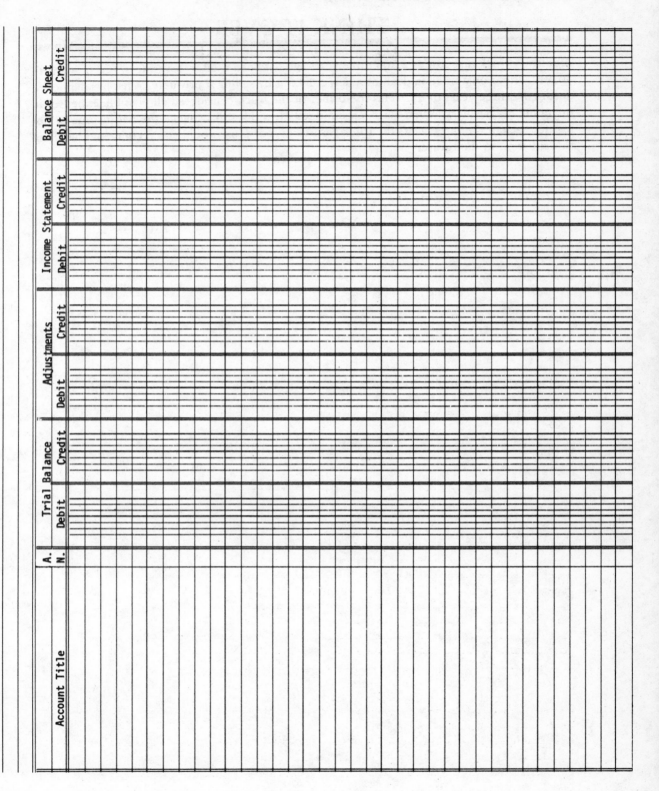

THINK IT OVER

A delivery truck that cost $12,500 three years ago has been used by a business. It is now worth $6,500, either on a trade-in deal for a new truck, or by selling it privately. What has happened during the three years of use? Has the owner of the truck considered all possible expenses in operating his business? What has been omitted? How does this change the net income or net loss for each of the three years the truck has been used? How would you recommend handling this situation in the future?

WORDS TO REMEMBER

Articles of Partnership the *written agreement* establishing a partnership

Cost of Goods Sold a section of the income statement that includes the *beginning inventory plus net purchases less the ending inventory*

Gross Profit the *difference* between *net income from sales* and *the cost of goods sold*

CHAPTER 19 FINANCIAL STATEMENTS

At the end of each fiscal period, financial statements are prepared to summarize the operations of a business. This information allows the owner(s) to see how profitable (or unprofitable) the business has been, to compare one fiscal period with prior periods, and to determine future courses of action. In addition, this information may be requested by banks, and by the Internal Revenue Service if tax returns are examined.

Income Statement

An INCOME STATEMENT describes the way in which a business has operated during a fiscal period. It is prepared from information on the work sheet in the special Income Statement columns. The income statement for Fields and Ross (see work sheet, page 173) follows:

Fields and Ross
Income Statement
For Year Ended December 31, 199–

Income:			
Sales		7600000	
Less Sales Returns and Allowances		175000	
Net Sales			7425000
Cost of Goods Sold:			
Merchandise Inv, Jan 1		1550000	
Purchases	30,000		
Less Purchases Returns			
and Allowances	580		
Net Purchases		2942000	
Merchandise Available for Sale		4492000	
Less Merchandise Inv, Dec. 31		1360000	
Cost of Goods Sold			3132000
Gross Profit on Sales			4293000
Expenses:			
Advertising Expense		120000	
Miscellaneous Expense		12000	
Rent Expense		240000	
Salary Expense		600000	
Supplies Expense		95000	
Total Expenses			1067000
Net Income			3226000

The customary three-line heading indicates the answers to WHO, WHAT, and WHEN. The statement is divided into five parts:

(1) An *income* section, listing all operating income earned during the fiscal period—sales, less sales returns and allowances.

Sales − Sales Returns and Allowances = Net Sales

(2) A *cost of goods sold* section, which includes the following: beginning inventory, plus net purchases (purchases, less purchases returns and allowances), less ending inventory.

Beginning Inventory + Net Purchases − Ending Inventory = Cost of Goods Sold

(3) The *gross profit*, which is the difference between net sales and cost of goods sold.

Net Sales − Cost of Goods Sold = Gross Profit

(4) The *expenses* section, listing all operating expenses for the fiscal period.
(5) The *net income*, which is the difference between gross profit on sales and total expenses.

Gross Profit − Total Expenses = Net Income (or Net Loss)

In the event that total expenses exceed gross profit on sales, the result is a net loss for the fiscal period.

Briefly stated, an income statement shows

Net Sales
− Cost of Goods Sold
= Gross Profit on Sales
− Total Expenses
= Net Income (or Net Loss)

An income statement for a business owned by a single owner does not differ from one for a business owned by two or more people.

Capital Statement

This information is included in the CAPITAL STATEMENT, which shows how each partner's owner's equity changed during the fiscal period.

There must be an agreement as to how partners are to share any net income or net loss. If Fields and Ross in our example share equally, each partner would receive $16,130 (one half of $32,260). If partners share in any other way, this must be clearly stated in the ARTICLES OF PARTNERSHIP, the written agreement establishing the business. Assume in the case of Fields and Ross that the agreement provides for the partners to share income and losses *in the ratio* of 3 to 2 (3:2). This means that Fields would receive three fifths ($\frac{3}{5}$) or 60%, and Ross two fifths ($\frac{2}{5}$) or 40%, of any net income or any net loss.

Fields's share of the net income is, therefore, $19,356 ($\frac{3}{5}$ or 60% of $32,260), and Ross's share is $12,904 ($\frac{2}{5}$ or 40% of $32,260).

Fields and Ross
Capital Statement
For Year Ended December 31, 199–

A. G. Fields:			
Beginning Balance, Jan. 1		11595 00	
Plus 3/5 of Net Income	19,356		
Less Withdrawals	12,000		
Net Increase in Capital		7356 00	
Ending Balance, Dec. 31			18951 00
B. W. Ross:			
Beginning Balance, Jan. 1		10610 00	
Plus: Additional Investment	2,000		
2/5 of Net Income	12,904		
	14,904		
Less Withdrawals	12,000		
Net Increase in Capital		2904 00	
Ending Balance, Dec. 31			13514 00
Total Owner's Equity, Dec. 31			32465 00

Examine the following capital statement for Lois Berlowitz, who had a loss for the fiscal period:

Lois Berlowitz
Capital Statement
For Six Months Ended June 30, 199–

Beginning Balance, Jan. 1			28765 00
Additional Investment			2500 00
			31265 00
Less: Net Loss		5200 00	
Withdrawals		6000 00	
Total Decrease in Capital			11200 00
Ending Balance, June 30			20065 00

Balance Sheet

The next financial statement to be prepared is a BALANCE SHEET. This shows the financial condition of a business at the end of the fiscal period. The form presented below is the REPORT FORM balance sheet, listing items (assets, liabilities, and owners' equity) vertically, one under the other. Notice, however, that the fundamental bookkeeping/accounting equation is maintained and is emphasized by double-ruling *total assets* and *total liabilities plus owners' equity.*

Fields and Ross
Balance Sheet
December 31, 199-

Assets			
Cash		2250 00	
Petty Cash		50 00	
Accounts Receivable		3175 00	
Merchandise Inventory		13600 00	
Equipment		15000 00	
Supplies		440 00	
Total Assets			34515 00
Liabilities			
Accounts Payable			2050 00
Owners' Equity			
A. G. Fields, Capital		18951 00	
B. W. Ross, Capital		13514 00	
Total Owners' Equity			32465 00
Total Liabilities and Owners' Equity			34515 00

YOU SHOULD REMEMBER

The income statement shows:

Net Sales
less Cost of Goods Sold
equals Gross Profit (or Loss)
less Total Expenses
equals Net Income (or Loss).

Increases in *owner's equity* are caused by investments and net income.
Decreases in *owner's equity* are caused by withdrawals and net loss.

KNOW YOUR VOCABULARY

Articles of partnership
Balance Sheet
Capital statement
Cost of goods sold
Gross profit
Income statement
Partnership
Report form balance sheet

QUESTIONS

1. What information is shown on each of the following?
   a) An income statement.
   b) A capital statement.
   c) A balance sheet.
2. How is the cost of goods sold calculated?
3. What determines whether there is a net income or a net loss for a fiscal period?
4. How does a report form balance sheet differ from an account form balance sheet?

PROBLEMS

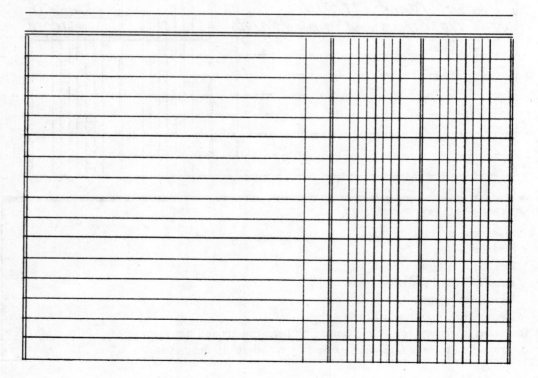

19–1 Using the completed work sheet for Daniel Green (Problem 18–1), complete:
1) An income statement.
2) A capital statement (assume that Green's capital includes a $2,000 additional investment).
3) A balance sheet.

1)

2)

3)

19–2 Using the completed work sheet for Timothy Sullivan (Problem 18–2), complete:
1) An income statement.
2) A capital statement (examine Sullivan's capital account for any additional investment; see pp. 178–181).
3) A balance sheet.

1)

2)

3)

19–3 Abdullah and Pahlevi are partners who share profits and losses in the ratio of 4:3. Their general ledger account balances at the end of the year are as follows:

Cash	$ 3,625
Accounts Receivable	18,260
Merchandise Inventory, January 1	22,320
Equipment	7,500
Prepaid Insurance	500
Supplies	275
Accounts Payable	3,105
T. G. Abdullah, Capital	33,802
T. G. Abdullah, Drawing	10,000
S. H. Pahlevi, Capital	28,404
S. H. Pahlevi, Drawing	12,000
Revenue and Expense Summary	– –
Sales	51,790
Sales Returns and Allowances	2,570
Purchases	31,380
Purchases Returns and Allowances	1,529
Advertising Expense	600
Insurance Expense	– –
Rent Expense	3,600
Salary Expense	6,000
Supplies Expense	– –

Additional Information, December 31:

Merchandise Inventory	$23,195
Prepaid Insurance	$400
Supplies on Hand	$178.50

Complete the following:

1) A work sheet.
2) An income statement.
3) A capital statement (assume that Abdullah made a $5,000 additional investment during the fiscal period, which was included in his capital account balance).
4) A balance sheet.

1)

Account Title	A. N.	Trial Balance		Adjustments		Income Statement		Balance Sheet	
		Debit	Credit	Debit	Credit	Debit	Credit	Debit	Credit

(2)

(3)

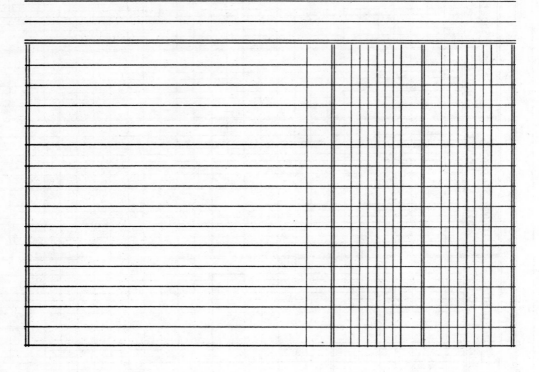

4) ____

THINK IT OVER

Paul Garrison believes his balance sheet does not reflect a correct end-of-fiscal-period financial condition. He is concerned because several of his charge customers (accounts receivable) have been unable to pay him amounts that are due. In past years, he has seen a similar situation: there are always some uncollectible accounts.

Does this situation affect the value of Garrison's assets? What adjustment might be made to account for an estimated loss on "bad debts" at the end of each fiscal period?

How would this adjustment affect Garrison's operating expenses if he estimates that approximately $500 may be uncollectible accounts receivable and, therefore, another operating expense? How would this affect Garrison's net income or net loss for the fiscal period?

WORDS TO REMEMBER

Adjusting Entries entries made first on a work sheet *to bring certain accounts up to date*, then journalized and posted to the general ledger

Closing Entries entries made at the end of a fiscal period *to "zero out" income, cost, expense, and drawing account balances*, so that this information will not be confused with similar information in future fiscal periods

Post-closing Trial Balance proof that the sum of general ledger account debit balances equals the sum of the general ledger account credit balances after posting all closing entries

CHAPTER 20

ADJUSTING AND CLOSING THE GENERAL LEDGER

In Chapters 18 and 19, work sheets with adjustments were completed, and certain accounts were brought up to date. These ADJUSTING ENTRIES reflected the changes that had taken place but had not been recorded in the actual accounts. *General ledger accounts* must now be brought up to date so that these changes become part of the permanent bookkeeping/accounting records.

Adjusting Accounts

Examine the Adjustments columns of the work sheet for Fields and Ross, page 173. Entries, with debits and credits identified by letters A, B, and C, pair off each adjustment. These are recorded in a general journal (using the General Dr. and General Cr. columns of a four-column general journal). The illustration below shows these adjusting entries *posted* to general ledger accounts.

GENERAL JOURNAL

Page 4

Accts. Pay. Dr.	General Dr.	Date		PR	General Cr.	Accts. Rec. Cr.
		199-	Adjusting Entries			
	15500 00	Dec. 31	Revenue and Expense Summary	313		
			Merchandise Inventory	114	15500 00	
	13600 00	31	Merchandise Inventory	114		
			Revenue and Expense Summary	313	13600 00	
	950 00	31	Supplies Expense	615		
			Supplies	116	950 00	

GENERAL LEDGER

Merchandise Inventory

No. 114

Date			PR	Dr.	Cr.	Balance Dr.	Balance Cr.
199- Jan.	1	Balance	✓			15500 00	
Dec.	31		J4		15500 00	—	
	31		J4	13600 00		13600 00	

Supplies

No. 116

Date			PR	Dr.	Cr.	Balance Dr.	Balance Cr.
199- Jan.	1	Balance	✓			500 00	
May	15		CP3	600 00		1100 00	
Nov.	3		CP8	290 00		1390 00	
Dec.	31		J4		950 00	440 00	

Revenue and Expense Summary — No. 313

Date			PR	Dr.	Cr.	Balance Dr.	Balance Cr.
199- Dec.	31		J4	15,500 00		15,500 00	
	31		J4		13,600 00	1,900 00	

Supplies Expense — No. 615

Date			PR	Dr.	Cr.	Balance Dr.	Balance Cr.
199- Dec.	31		J4	950 00		950 00	

The ledger Posting Reference column indicates postings from general journal page 4 (J4). These accounts—Merchandise Inventory, Supplies, and Supplies Expense—are now up to date.

Closing Accounts

The next step at the end of the fiscal period is the closing procedure. Examine once again the Fields and Ross work sheet, page 173. The accounts listed in the Income Statement columns—all *revenue, cost, and expense accounts*, and the *Revenue and Expense Summary account*—and, in the Balance Sheet debit column, the *drawing accounts* are temporary accounts that are to be closed or "zeroed out." The information they show is for one fiscal period only and does not carry over to succeeding periods. CLOSING ENTRIES will close these temporary accounts.

First, close the accounts listed in the Income Statement credit column. They are *debited* to "zero out," and their total is *credited* to Revenue and Expense Summary.

Second, close the accounts listed in the Income Statement debit column. They are *credited* to "zero out," and their total is *debited* to Revenue and Expense Summary.

Third, close the Revenue and Expense Summary account. The amount of *net income* is *debited* to Revenue and Expense Summary to "zero out" and is *credited* to the owners' capital accounts. (Had there been a *net loss*, the debits and credits would have been reversed.)

Fourth, close the drawing accounts. Owners' capital accounts are *debited*, and their drawing accounts are *credited* to "zero out."

Closing entries continue in the general journal, immediately following the adjusting entries:

Debit	Date	Account	Credit
		Closing Entries	
76000 00	31	Sales	
580 00		Purchases Returns and Allows.	
		Revenue and Expense Summary	76580 00
42420 00	31	Revenue and Expense Summary	
		Sales Returns and Allowances	1750 00
		Purchases	30000 00
		Advertising Expense	1200 00
		Miscellaneous Expense	120 00
		Rent Expense	2400 00
		Salary Expense	6000 00
		Supplies Expense	950 00
32260 00	31	Revenue and Expense Summary	
		A. G. Fields, Capital	19356 00
		B. W. Ross, Capital	12904 00
12000 00	31	A. G. Fields, Capital	
12000 00		B. W. Ross, Capital	
		A. G. Fields, Drawing	12000 00
		B. W. Ross, Drawing	12000 00

These entries are then posted to the general ledger.

Post-Closing Trial Balance

To prove that the adjusting and closing work has been completed correctly, a last POST-CLOSING TRIAL BALANCE is taken. The accounts that are open at this point will have balances that carry over to succeeding fiscal periods. These are balance sheet accounts—*assets, liabilities*, and *capital*. Below is the post-closing trial balance for Fields and Ross. (If a complete general ledger had been illustrated here, all of these account balances would now be apparent, and they would be the source of the information listed.)

Fields and Ross
Post-closing Trial Balance
December 31, 199-

Cash	2250 00	
Petty Cash	50 00	
Accounts Receivable	3175 00	
Merchandise Inventory	13600 00	
Equipment	15000 00	
Supplies	440 00	
Accounts Payable		2050 00
A. G. Fields, Capital		18951 00
B. W. Ross, Capital		13514 00
	34515 00	34515 00

YOU SHOULD REMEMBER

Adjusting and closing entries are not transactions; they are the bookkeeper's way of first *bringing accounts up to date, and then zeroing out income, cost, expense and drawing account balances* at the end of each fiscal period.

A post-closing trial balance lists only accounts which have *balances that carry over to the succeeding fiscal period.*

KNOW YOUR VOCABULARY

- Adjusting entry
- Closing Entry
- Post-closing trial balance

QUESTIONS

1. How are debits and credits for each adjustment shown on the work sheet?
2. Why is it necessary to journalize and post adjusting entries, inasmuch as they are included on the work sheet?
3. Which columns of the work sheet contain information needed for journalizing closing entries?
4. What does the first closing entry accomplish?
5. What does the second closing entry accomplish?
6. What is the third closing entry when there has been a net income for the fiscal period? A net loss for the fiscal period?

7. How does the posting of the third closing entry affect the owner's equity?
8. How does the posting of the fourth closing entry affect the owner's equity?
9. Why are balance sheet accounts the only accounts listed on a post-closing trial balance?
10. What does the post-closing trial balance prove?

PROBLEMS

20–1 Refer to Problem 18–1. Using a four-column general journal, page 7, complete the following:

1) The adjusting entries.
2) The closing entries.

(1) and (2)

GENERAL JOURNAL — Page

Acct. Pay. Dr.	General Dr.	Date		PR	General Cr.	Acct. Rec. Cr.

20–2 Refer to Problem 18–2. Using a two-column general journal, page 6, do the following:

1) Record the adjusting entries and post.
2) Record the closing entries and post.
3) Take a post-closing trial balance.

(1) and (2)

GENERAL JOURNAL

Page

Date		Account Title	PR	Debit	Credit

(3)

20–3 Refer to Problem 19–3. Using a four-column general journal, page 9, do the following:

1) **Record the adjusting entries.**
2) **Record the closing entries.**

(1) and (2)

GENERAL JOURNAL — Page

Acct. Pay. Dr.	General Dr.	Date		PR	General Cr.	Acct. Rec. Cr.

3) Can you prepare a post-closing trial balance from the information in this problem, even though you have no ledger? If so, how? See solution and explain how each account balance was found.

WORDS TO REMEMBER

Combination Journal a columnar book in which general and special (cash receipts, cash disbursements, sales, purchases, entries, etc.) are combined

Verify Cash Balance a procedure in which the beginning balance, plus the cash debit total, less the cash credit total is compared with the balance of cash on hand or in the bank (which it should equal)

CHAPTER 21 USING A COMBINATION JOURNAL

In chapters 1–20, basic bookkeeping and accounting principles were developed. These may be applied to personal as well as business use. Some individuals and many small businesses prefer to use the simplest forms possible. This can be accomplished using a COMBINATION JOURNAL, a columnar book which combines a general journal with whatever special journals—cash receipts, cash disbursements, sales, and purchases—may be needed.

Combination Journal For Personal Use

The arrangement of columns will differ from one individual to another. Most, however, will have special columns for cash receipts (Cash Dr.) and cash disbursements (Cash Cr.) as well as two general columns (General Dr. and General Cr.)

Examine carefully the combination journal below for Alan Daniels:

COMBINATION JOURNAL

p. 3

Cash Dr.		Cash Cr.		Date		Explanation / Account	PR	General Dr.		General Cr.	
				199– May	1	Balance on hand 675–	✓				
600	00				5	Salary Income				600	00
		76	90		8	Stern's (charge acct.)		76	90		
		12	50		10	Auto Expense (gas)		12	50		
		275	00		31	Insurance Expense		275	00		
2400 00 2400	00	2175 40 2175	40		31	Totals		2175 40 2175	40	2400 00 2400	00
(	)	(	)					(✓	)	(✓	)

At the end of the month, Daniels can verify his cash balance by adding the beginning balance and the cash debit total, less the cash credit total:

$$
\begin{array}{r}
675.00 \\
+\ \underline{2400.00} \\
3075.00 \\
-\ \underline{2175.40} \\
899.60
\end{array}
$$

899.60—This amount should equal his balance of cash on hand and/or in the bank.

Note that pencil footings are used to prove the debit column totals equal the credit column totals, *before* those amounts are written in ink. If Daniels posts to ledger accounts, the cash *totals* are posted as the column headings indicate (Dr. and Cr.) and *each item* in the general debit and credit columns is posted to the account identified in the explanation column. The general column totals *are not* posted.

Combination Journal For Business Use

Depending upon their need, the arrangement of columns will differ from one business to another. Most combination journals will include special columns for cash receipts (Cash Dr.) and cash disbursements (Cash Cr.) as well as two general columns (General Dr. and General Cr.). In addition, there may be special columns for customers' accounts (Accounts Receivable Dr. and Cr.), sales of merchandise (Sales Cr.), creditors' accounts (Accounts Payable Dr. and Cr.), and purchases of merchandise (Purchases Dr.).

If similar transactions occur frequently in a relatively short time, a special column may be used for that account. An example of this might be for the purchase of supplies used in a business (Supplies Dr. or Supplies Expense Dr.)

Examine carefully the combination journal opposite for Karen and Kenneth's Promotional's business:

COMBINATION JOURNAL

p. 5

General		Date		Explanation	PR	Cash		Accounts Receivable		Sales	Accounts Payable		Purchases	Supplies
Dr.	Cr.					Dr.	Cr.	Dr.	Cr.	Credit	Dr.	Cr.	Dr.	Dr.
		199- May	1	Balance 1500.00	✓									
			3	Thomas Co.		500 00			500 00					
			6	Wiley Inc.				750 00		750 00				
			8	Supplies	✓		40 00							40 00
250 00			10	Equipment			250 00							
			15	H.K. Mfg. Co.								350 00	350 00	
			20	Sales	✓	1500 00				1500 00				
600 00			31	Rent Expense			600 00							
1790 00	50 00		31	Totals		4750 00	2900 00	2100 00	2980 00	3950 00	800 00	850 00	950 00	340 00
(✓)	(✓)					( )	( )	( )	( )	( )	( )	( )	( )	( )

Note that footii gs are used to prove the equality of debits and credits:

Debits—

General	1,790.00
Cash	4,750.00
Accts. Rec.	2,100.00
Accts. Pay.	800.00
Purchases	950.00
Supplies	340.00
	10,730.00

Credits—

General	50.00
Cash	2,900.00
Accts. Rec.	2,980.00
Sales	3,950.00
Accts. Pay.	850.00
	10,730.00

Totals are then written in ink and double-lined. All special column totals are to be posted, indicated by open parentheses, to the accounts indicated in the column headings. Items that are check-marked are not to be posted—the general debit and credit column totals and any accounts in the explanation column for which there are special columns.

It is assumed there are subsidiary ledgers for customers' and creditors' accounts. Since these accounts are arranged alphabetically, a check mark will be entered in the posting reference column as each one is posted.

Verify Cash Balance

The bookkeeper verifies the cash balance by adding the beginning balance and the cash debit total, less the cash credit total:

	1,500.00
+	4,750.00
	6,250.00
−	2,900.00
	3,350.00—This amount should equal the balance

of cash on hand and/or in the bank.

YOU SHOULD REMEMBER

A combination journal replaces special journals to simplify bookkeeping procedures. All transactions are entered in one journal.

Columnar headings and arrangement will vary from one individual and/or business to another.

For every entry, bookkeeping/accounting double-entry theory applies. The amount(s) debited equal the amount(s) credited. In that way, if the journal is properly proved and posted, a trial balance should be in balance.

KNOW YOUR VOCABULARY

Combination Journal   Verify Cash Balance

QUESTIONS

1. What determines which accounts will be used as special columns?
2. Which transactions will be check-marked as they are entered in a combination journal?
3. How is a combination journal proved?
4. Which column totals are posted?
5. Which column totals are not to be posted?

PROBLEMS

21–1 Dana and Marvin Manross use a combination journal for their family records. They have decided to use special columns — one for all household operating expenses, and another for all automobile expenses. On May 1st, their balance of cash on hand and in the bank was $1,675.00.

(1) Record the following transactions:

May 1, 199–	Paid the rent, $695.00
3,	Paid for personal expenses, $37.95
5,	Gas for their car, $14.60
8,	Electricity bill, $79.50
10,	Food shopping, $63.45
12,	Quarterly premium on household insurance, $108.75
15,	Two weeks' salary, cash received, $1,048.30
21,	Automobile insurance for year, $355.20
24,	Food shopping, $59.25
25,	Personal expenses, $48.95
26,	Automobile tune-up, $66.50
28,	Medical bill, $80.00
29,	Two weeks' salary, cash received, $1,048.30
30,	Paid charge accounts, $91.85
31,	Telephone bill, $54.30

(2) Summarize the journal.

(3) Verify cash balance on May 31.

21–1

COMBINATION JOURNAL

General		Date	Explanation	PR	Cash		House.	Auto
Dr.	Cr.				Dr.	Cr.	Exp. Dr.	Exp. Dr.

21–2 Antonina and Salvatore Moffo use a combination journal for their personal household records. Because Mrs. Moffo is a diabetic and under a doctor's care, they use a special column for medical expenses, as well as one for their home and food expenses.

(1) Record their transactions for the month:

June 1, Cash balance on hand and in the bank, $1,162.00
1, Paid month's rent, $900
2, Food shopping, $68.75
4, Movies and refreshments, $16.50
5, Gas and electric bill, $96.25
8, Doctor's visit, $45 and medication, $22.50
12, Food shopping, $72.50
15, Visited local museum, $6.00 and went to dinner, $32.45
19, Doctor's visit, $45 and lab fees, $30
22, Telephone bill, $42.92
25, Food shopping, $61.47
27, Paid charge account, Stern Bros., $52.50
29, Donation to the Diabetes Foundation, $25.00
30, Monthly pay check, $2,400.00
30, Movies and refreshments, $15.00

(2) Summarize the journal.

(3) Verify the cash balance, June 30.

21–2

COMBINATION JOURNAL

General		Date	Account / Explanation	PR	Cash		House.	Medical
Dr.	Cr.				Dr.	Cr.	Exp. Dr.	Exp. Dr.

21–3 Paula Davis is an attorney who uses a combination journal for her law practice's bookkeeping records. She uses special columns for cash (Cash Dr. and Cash Cr.), her clients (Accounts Receivable Dr. and Accounts Receivable Cr.), her income from legal fees (Fees Income Cr.), and the major categories of expenditures (Office Expenses Dr. and Travel and Auto Expenses Dr.).

(1) Record the following transactions:

June 1, Cash balance on hand and in bank, $1,042.35
1, Paid office rent, $650.00
3, Paid for stationery and cards, $32.90
5, Settled H. L. Thompson case. Client awarded $12,000 in damages. Davis will receive $33\frac{1}{3}\%$ plus reimbursed expenses, $362.40 (Debit Accounts Receivable and credit Fees Income.)
8, Purchased from Apex Furniture Company a desk and two chairs, $2,250; cash deposit $750, balance on account
11, Paid telephone bill, $67.88
15, Paid for legal forms, $28.25
20, Tolls and mileage to visit a client, $16.50
22, Received cash for settlement in Thompson case
24, Purchased new file cabinet for cash, $350.00
27, Paid for postage, $10.00
29, Paid for gasoline, $14.00
30, Davis withdrew for personal use, $1,200.00
30, Returned defective file cabinet; received full refund

(2) Summarize the journal.

(3) Verify cash balance on June 30.

21–3 (1) and (2)

COMBINATION JOURNAL

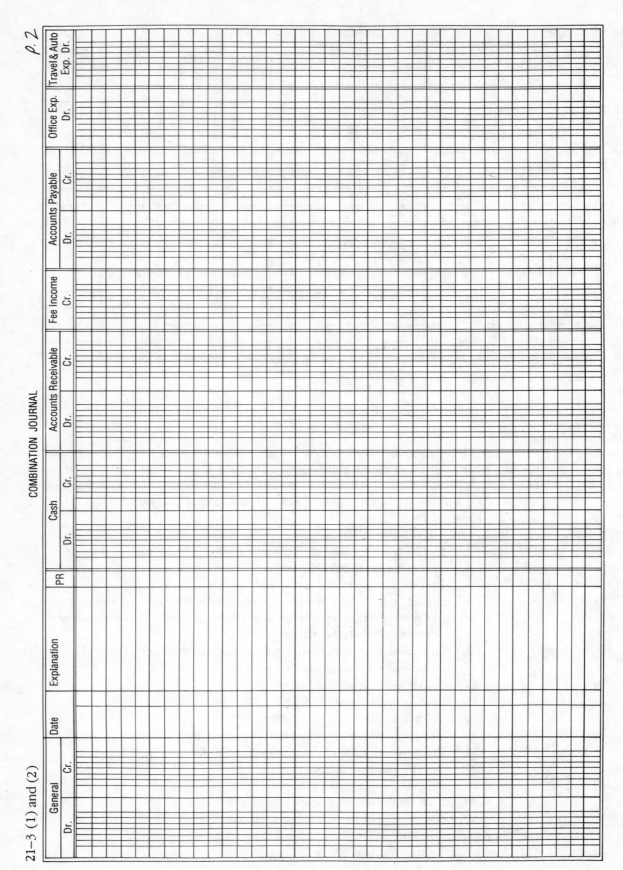

p. 2

General		Date	Explanation	PR	Cash		Accounts Receivable		Fee Income	Accounts Payable		Office Exp.	Travel & Auto
Dr.	Cr.				Dr.	Cr.	Dr.	Cr.	Cr.	Dr.	Cr.	Dr.	Exp. Dr.

21–4 Chris Bayer and Lee Falk are partners who use a combination journal for their wholesale business.

(1) Record the following transactions for the month of June:

June 1, Cash balance on hand and in the bank, $5,162.00
1, Paid rent for the month, $1,200.00
3, Sales on account to Smythe Co., $1,950.00
5, Paid on account Maxwell Inc., $1,600.00
8, Received cash on account from PVP & Co., $995.00
12, Purchased merchandise on account from Khan & Farah, $3,000.00
13, Bought office supplies, $62.50
15, Paid salaries, $2,000.00
19, Received cash on account from Bill Bros., $1,535.50
21, Paid for advertising in trade journal, $125.00
24, Each partner withdrew cash for personal use, $350.00
27, Purchased merchandise from Peck & Persky Inc., $1,500.00
29, Paid on account Khan & Farah, $1,000.00
30, Paid telephone bill, $182.75
30, Received on account from Smythe Co., $1,950.00
30, Sold an office desk and chair; received $250.00

(2) Summarize the journal, and prove the equality of debits and credits.

(3) Rule the combination journal. Check mark any column totals that should not be posted.

(4) What is the cash balance on June 30?

21–4

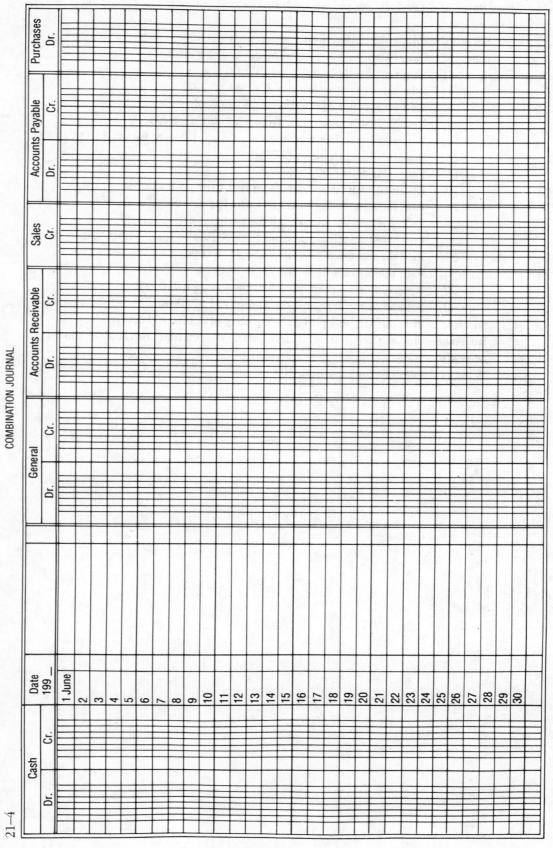

COMBINATION JOURNAL

Cash		Date			General		Accounts Receivable		Sales	Accounts Payable		Purchases
Dr.	Cr.	199 __			Dr.	Cr.	Dr.	Cr.	Cr.	Dr.	Cr.	Dr.
		1 June										
		2										
		3										
		4										
		5										
		6										
		7										
		8										
		9										
		10										
		11										
		12										
		13										
		14										
		15										
		16										
		17										
		18										
		19										
		20										
		21										
		22										
		23										
		24										
		25										
		26										
		27										
		28										
		29										
		30										

CYCLE TWO EXAMINATION

Part I Indicate by a check (✓) in the column at the right whether each statement is TRUE or FALSE.

	Statement		T	F
Example:	Debts owed to creditors are accounts payable.		✓	
1.	A purchases journal is used for recording the purchase of all merchandise on account.	1.		
2.	Cost accounts increase by debits.	2.		
3.	A major advantage of special journals is the elimination of repetitive posting.	3.		
4.	A source document for each transaction is identified in the ledger account.	4.		
5.	A controlling account is found in each subsidiary ledger.	5.		
6.	A summary entry proves that debits equal credits in each journal.	6.		
7.	A check-mark posting reference to a customer's account indicates that the item has been posted.	7.		
8.	General Debit and General Credit column totals are posted to general ledger accounts.	8.		
9.	A subsidiary ledger's accuracy is proved by taking a trial balance.	9.		
10.	Invoices usually are prepared in multiple copies.	10.		
11.	The use of special journals eliminates the need for controlling accounts.	11.		
12.	A correcting entry usually is recorded in the general journal.	12.		
13.	A charge to the wrong customer's account is corrected by debiting that account and crediting the correct one.	13.		
14.	A withdrawal of merchandise by the owner is debited to the Sales account.	14.		
15.	A statement of account is sent to each charge customer to indicate the balance due.	15.		
16.	An eight-column work sheet includes special columns for closing entries.	16.		
17.	Prepaid expenses are adjusted at the end of each fiscal period by the amounts of their ending inventory values.	17.		
18.	Partners automatically share net income equally unless a written agreement specifies otherwise.	18.		
19.	Gross profit on sales is found by subtracting cost of goods sold from net sales.	19.		
20.	A post-closing trial balance includes general ledger accounts with adjusted balances.	20.		

Part II Match the definition with the term by writing the appropriate letter in the column at the right. (A term is used once only.)

Terms	Definitions		Letter
	Example: A charge purchase of merchandise, rather than a purchase for cash		K
A. Adjusting entries	1. A special grouping of similar accounts	1.	
B. Capital statement	2. A source document that describes a sale of merchandise	2.	
C. Cash disbursement	3. The totaling of all special journals to prove that debits equal credits	3.	
D. Cash receipts journal	4. A special journal for all cash payments	4.	
E. Closing entries	5. The journal in which a withdrawal of merchandise by the owner is recorded.	5.	
F. Debit G. Credit	6. The normal balance of a customer's account	6.	
H. General journal	7. A valuation account	7.	
I. Income statement	8. Entries made at the end of the fiscal period to bring certain accounts up to date	8.	
J. Invoice K. On account	9. The financial statement that shows changes in owner's equity	9.	
L. Purchases returns and allowances	10. Proving that general ledger debits and credits are equal	10.	
M. Subsidiary ledger			
N. Summary entry			
O. Trial balance			

Part III (1) Record each of the following transactions for Rex Drug Company in the journals provided:

June 1, Paid month's rent, $375; check No. 147
3, Purchased $500 worth of merchandise on account from J. L. Rossini Company
5, Sold merchandise on account to Dr. George Tyler, $165
8, The owner, Howard Craven, withdrew $50 worth of merchandise for personal use
10, Paid J. L. Rossini Company $500 on account; check No. 148
12, Issued credit memo No. 7 for $15 to Dr. George Tyler for merchandise returned
15, Cash sales to date were $2,950
19, Paid telephone bill, $46; check No. 149
22, Received $150 from Dr. George Tyler for balance due on account
26, Sold $125 worth of merchandise to Mel Guberman on account
29, Purchased $300 worth of merchandise from Fred Pulaski Wholesalers, Inc., on account
30, Cash sales to date were $3,750

(2) Summarize each journal, and checkmark any totals not to be posted.

1) and 2)

GENERAL JOURNAL Page 3

Accts.Pay. Dr.	General Dr.	Date		PR	General Cr.	Accts. Rec. Cr.

1) and 2)

PURCHASES JOURNAL

Page 2

Date	Account Credited			PR	Purchases Dr. Accts. Pay. Cr.

1) and 2)

SALES JOURNAL

Page 4

Date	Account Debited		PR	Acct. Rec. Dr. Sales Cr.

1) and 2)

CASH RECEIPTS JOURNAL — Page 3

Date			PR	General Cr.	Accts. Rec. Cr.	Sales Cr.	Cash Dr.
199- June	1	Balance on hand $2,500	✓				

(1) and (2)

CASH DISBURSEMENTS JOURNAL

Page 3

Date	Account Debited	Ck. No.	PR	General Dr.	Accts. Pay. Dr.	Purchases Dr.	Salary Exp. Dr.	Cash Cr.

Part IV From the completed work sheet below do the following:

(1) Prepare an income statement.

(2) Complete a capital statement, assuming that Fowler made a $1,000 investment during the fiscal period.

(3) Prepare a balance sheet.

(4) Journalize the adjusting and closing entries.

Fowler's Crystal Palace
Work Sheet
For Year Ended December 31, 199-

Account Title	A. N.	Trial Balance Debit	Trial Balance Credit	Adjustments Debit	Adjustments Credit	Income Statement Debit	Income Statement Credit	Balance Sheet Debit	Balance Sheet Credit
Cash	111	2400 00						2400 00	
Accounts Receivable	112	3850 00						3850 00	
Merchandise Inventory	113	10790 00		(B) 12080 00	(A) 10790 00			12080 00	
Furniture and Fixtures	114	8500 00						8500 00	
Prepaid Insurance	115	600 00			(C) 500 00			100 00	
Supplies	116	325 00			(D) 220 00			105 00	
Accounts Payable	211		4500 00						4500 00
Dina Fowler, Capital	311		26525 00						26525 00
Dina Fowler, Drawing	312	12000 00						12000 00	
Revenue and Expense Summary	313			(A) 10790 00	(B) 12080 00	10790 00	12080 00		
Sales	411		40590 00				40590 00		
Sales Returns and Allowances	411.1	1875 00				1875 00			
Purchases	511	21630 00				21630 00			
Purchases Returns and Allowances	511.1		795 00				795 00		
Advertising Expense	611	1200 00				1200 00			
Insurance Expense	612			(C) 500 00		500 00			
Miscellaneous Expense	613	240 00				240 00			
Rent Expense	614	3000 00				3000 00			
Salary Expense	615	6000 00				6000 00			
Supplies Expense	316			(D) 220 00		220 00			
		72410 00	72410 00	23590 00	23590 00	45455 00	53465 00	39035 00	31025 00
Net Income						8010 00			8010 00
						53465 00	53465 00	39035 00	39035 00

(1)

(2)

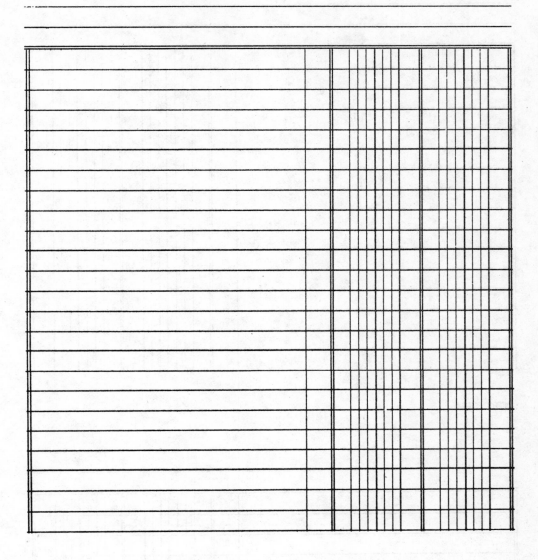

(3)

(EXTRA FORM)

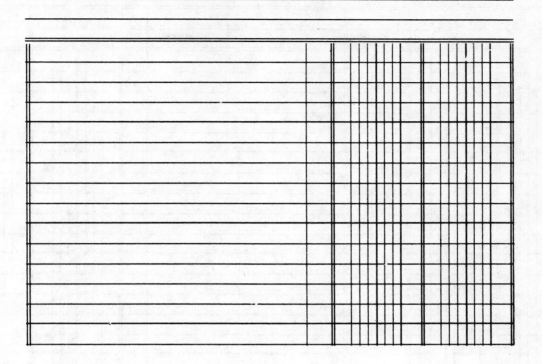

(4)

GENERAL JOURNAL

Page

Accts. Pay. Dr.	General Dr.	Date		PR	General Cr.	Accts. Rec. Cr.

GENERAL JOURNAL Page

Accts. Pay. Dr.	General Dr.	Date		PR	General Cr.	Accts. Rec. Cr.

ANSWERS TO SELECTED QUESTIONS AND PROBLEMS

Chapter 1

1–1

1.	$ 11,500.00
2.	3,700.00
3.	17,500.00
4.	16,087.10
5.	8,569.07
6.	106,930.96
7.	210,818.34
8.	40,314.48
9.	571,657.75
10.	1,116,743.28

Chapter 2

QUESTIONS

	Classification	Side
1.	Asset	Left
2.	Liability	Right
3.	Owner's equity	Right
4.	Asset	Left
5.	Liability	Right
6.	Asset	Left
7.	Asset	Left
8.	Liability	Right
9.	Asset	Left
10.	Owner's equity	Right

PROBLEMS

2–1	*A* =	*L* +	*OE*
1.	Decrease	Decrease	
2.	None		
3.	Increase	Increase	
4.	None		
5.	None		
6.	Increase		Increase
7.	None		
8.	Decrease		Decrease

2–2

	A	= L	+ OE
1.	−$ 2,000		
	+ 2,000		
	$29,250	$ 4,250	$25,000
2.	+ 7,500	+ 7,500	
	$36,750	$11,750	$25,000
3.	−$ 450		
	+ 450		
	$36,750	$11,750	$25,000
4.	−$12,000		
	+ 12,000		
	$36,750	$11,750	$25,000
5.	− 1,500	− 1,500	
	$35,250	$10,250	$25,000

Chapter 3

3–1

	Classification
1.	Asset
2.	Liability
3.	Asset
4.	Owner's equity
5.	Asset
6.	Asset
7.	Liability
8.	Liability
9.	Owner's equity
10.	Liability

3–2

	Left Side	Right Side
1.	Asset	
2.		Liability
3.	Asset	
4.		Liability
5.	Asset	
6.	Asset	
7.	Asset	
8.		Owner's equity
9.	Asset	
10.		Owner's equity

3–3

Maria's Beauty Salon
Balance Sheet
August 31, 199-

Assets		Liabilities	
Cash	1750 00	Regal Laundry	275 00
Furn. & Fixtures	8900 00	Marvelle Corp.	2500 00
Beauty Supplies	600 00	Total Liab.	2775 00
		Owner's Equity	
		Maria Lopez, Cap.	8475 00
Total Assets	11250 00	Total Liab. & OE	11250 00

3–4 Total Assets, $7,685

Total Liabilities,	$ 825
Capital	6,860
Total Liab. + OE	$7,685

3–5 Total Assets, $1,389.50

Total Liabilities,	$ 197.75
Capital	1,191.75
Total Liab. + OE	$1,389.50

3–6 Total Assets, $104,050

Total Liabilities,	$ 28,925.00
Capital	75,125.00
Total Liab. + OE	$104,050.00

Chapter 4

4–1 (2) Total Assets, $5,345

Total Liabilities,	$ 575
Capital	4,770
Total Liab. + OE	$5,345

Therefore:

Emilee Suzanne, Capital	
	4770

4–2 (2) Total Assets, $7,910

Total Liabilities,	$2,050
Capital	5,860
Total Liab. + OE	$7,910

4–5 (3) Total Assets, $3,682.50

Total Liabilities,	$ 215.00
Capital	3,467.50
Total Liab. + OE	$3,682.50

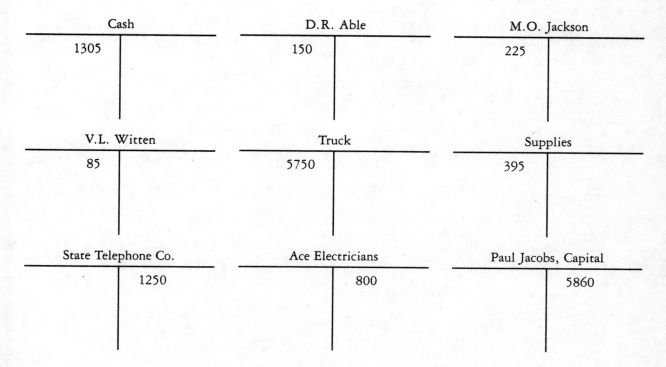

4–2 (1)

Cash	
1305	

D.R. Able	
150	

M.O. Jackson	
225	

V.L. Witten	
85	

Truck	
5750	

Supplies	
395	

State Telephone Co.	
	1250

Ace Electricians	
	800

Paul Jacobs, Capital	
	5860

4–3

Cash

Debit		Credit	
	4075	*Ex.*	150
(2)	1000	(1)	75
(3)	2500		

Equipment

Debit		Credit
	12500	
(4)	500	

Supplies

Debit		Credit
	200	
(1)	75	

Regal Bank Company

Debit		Credit	
Ex.	150		2000
		(2)	1000

Bixby Company

Debit	Credit	
	(4)	500

Kimberley Travis, Capital

Debit	Credit	
		21365
	(3)	2500

Chapter 5

5–1

Cash	377.00
Taxis	28000.00
Supplies	150.00
Salary Expense	200.00
Gas and Oil Expense	45.00
Puccio, Drawing	300.00
Repair Expense	40.00
Total	29112.00
Landia	6300.00
Puccio, Capital	22237.00
Fare Income	575.00
Total	29112.00

5–2 (1)

Cash	902.00
Accounts Receivable	425.00
Delivery Equipment	12000.00
Supplies	160.00
Tucker, Drawing	600.00
Advertising Expense	95.00
Telephone Expense	140.00
Trucking Expense	150.00
Total	14472.00
Accounts Payable	1075.00
Tucker, Capital	12297.00
Delivery Income	1100.00
Total	14472.00

5–2 (2) Total Assets, $13,487

Total Liabilities,	$ 1,075
Capital	12,412
Total Liab. + OE	$13,487

5–1
(1) and (2)

Cash

562	(b) 100
(a) 250	(c) 200
(e) 325	(d) 300
	(f) 45
	(g) 75
	(h) 40

Taxis

28000	

Supplies

150	

Landia National Bank

(b) 100	6400

Wilson Garage

(g) 75	75

Frank Puccio, Cap.

	22237

Frank Puccio, Drawing

(d) 300	

Fare Income

	(a) 250
	(e) 325

Gas & Oil Expense

(f) 45	

Repairs Expense

(h) 40	

Salary Expense

(c) 200	

Chapter 6

6–1

JOURNAL Page 7

Date		Account Title	PR	Debit	Credit
199- Oct.	2	Salary Expense		175 00	
		Cash			175 00
		Employee's Salary			
	7	Cash		600 00	
		Design Income			600 00
		Received for a design			
	14	Supplies		200 00	
		Cash			200 00
		Supplies and material			
	16	Cash		1000 00	
		Vernon Trust Co.			1000 00
		Borrowed from bank			
	21	Cash		500 00	
		Design Income			500 00
		Received for a design			
	23	Equipment		360 00	
		Cash			160 00
		Textile Equipment Co.			200 00
		new drawing table			
	30	Rose Klein, Drawing		400 00	
		Cash			400 00
		Withdrawal			
	31	Cash		100 00	
		Mary Wu			100 00
		Received on account			

Chapter 7

7–1 (ledger postings only)

Cash No. 11

Date		Item	P.R.	Debit	Date		Item	P.R.	Credit
199- Oct.	1	Balance	✓	1750 00	199- Oct.	18		6	500 00
	10		6	2500 00		25		6	250 00

Equipment No. 12

Date		Item	P.R.	Debit	Date		Item	P.R.	Credit
199- Oct.	1	Balance	✓	3000 00					
	1		6	1000 00					

Landers Mfg. Company No. 21

Date		Item	P.R.	Debit	Date		Item	P.R.	Credit
199- Oct.	25		6	250 00	199- Oct.	1		6	1000 00

L. D. Berger, Drawing No. 32

Date		Item	P.R.	Debit	Date		Item	P.R.	Credit
199- Oct.	18		6	500 00					

Service Income No. 41

Date		Item	P.R.	Debit	Date		Item	P.R.	Credit
					199- Oct.	10		6	2500 00

7–2

Cash	2020.00
Equipment	3965.00
Supplies	60.00
Kriss, Drawing	500.00
Advertising Expense	100.00
Utilities Expense	50.00
Total	6695.00
Hi-Tech	1925.00
Comp-Software	465.00
Kriss, Capital	3060.00
Services Income	1245.00
Total	6695.00

7–3

Cash	1275.00
Equipment	1642.50
Supplies	355.00
Schaffer, Drawing	300.00
Miscellaneous Expense	65.00
Total	3637.50
Jessup Bank	825.00
Schaffer, Capital	2372.50
Fee Income	440.00
Total	3637.50

7–3 (4)

Anita Schaffer
Trial Balance
October 31, 199-

Account	Debit	Credit
Cash	1 275 00	
Equipment	1 642 50	
Supplies	355 00	
Anita Schaffer, Drawing	300 00	
Miscellaneous Expense	65 00	
Jessup Bank		825 00
Anita Schaffer, Capital		2 372 50
Fee Income		440 00
	3 637 50	3 637 50

Chapter 8

8–2 (2) Trial Balance total, $7,251.40
8–2 (3) Net Income, $1,450
8–3 (1) Trial Balance total, $11,777.50
8–3 (2) Net Income, $1,150.50

8–1

J. R. Price
Work Sheet
For Month Ended November 30, 199–

Account Title	A. N.	Trial Balance Dr.	Trial Balance Cr.	Income Statement Dr.	Income Statement Cr	Balance Sheet Dr.	Balance Sheet Cr.
Cash		2645 00				2645 00	
Equipment		1500 00				1500 00	
Truck		7500 00				7500 00	
County Mfg. Co.			550 00				550 00
J. R. Price, Capital			10570 00				10570 00
J. R. Price, Drawing		500 00				500 00	
Commissions Income			1650 00		1650 00		
Advertising Expense		100 00		100 00			
Miscellaneous Expense		50 00		50 00			
Rent Expense		175 00		175 00			
Salary Expense		300 00		300 00			
		12770 00	12770 00	625 00	1650 00	12145 00	11120 00
Net Income				1025 00			1025 00
				1650 00	1650 00	12145 00	12145 00

8–3 (2)

Gayle's Reliable Service
Trial Balance
October 31, 199–

Account Title	A. N.	Trial Balance Debit	Trial Balance Credit	Income Statement Debit	Income Statement Credit	Balance Sheet Debit	Balance Sheet Credit
Cash		760 00				760 00	
Accounts Receivable		142 50				142 50	
Automobile		9200 00				9200 00	
Supplies		350 00				350 00	
County Bank & Trust Co.			3600 00				3600 00
Rebecca Gayle, Capital			6302 00				6302 00
Rebecca Gayle, Drawing		600 00				600 00	
Service Income			1875 50		1875 50		
Advertising Expense		200 00		200 00			
Auto Expense		400 00		400 00			
Miscellaneous Expense		50 00		50 00			
Telephone Expense		75 00		75 00			
		11777 50	11777 50	725 00	1875 50	11052 50	9902 00
Net Income				1150 50			1150 50
				1875 50	1875 50	11052 50	11052 50

Chapter 9

9–1 (a)

J. R. Price
Income Statement
For Month Ended November 30, 199–

Revenue:		
Commissions Income		1650 00
Expenses:		
Advertising Expense	100 00	
Miscellaneous Expense	50 00	
Rent Expense	175 00	
Salary Expense	300 00	
Total Expenses		625 00
Net Income		1025 00

9–1 (b)

J. R. Price
Capital Statement
For Month Ended November 30, 199–

Beginning Balance, Nov. 1, 199–		10570.00
Plus: Net Income	1025.00	
Less: Withdrawals	500.00	
Net Increase in Capital		525.00
Ending Balance, Nov. 30, 199–		11095.00

9–1 (c)

J. R. Price
Balance Sheet
November 30, 199–

Assets		Liabilities	
Cash	2645.00	County Mfg. Company	550.00
Equipment	1500.00	Owners' Equity	
Truck	7500.00	J. R. Price, Capital, Nov. 30	11095.00
Total Assets	11645.00	Total Liab. + O.E.	11645.00

9–2 (b) $4,901.40

9–3 (b) Capital, October 31, 199–, $6,852.50

9–4 (1) Trial Balance totals:

5648.00	8600.00
10400.00	28243.00
420.00	3680.00
2655.00	40523.00
15000.00	
400.00	
1500.00	
2500.00	
800.00	
1200.00	
40523.00	

Net Loss, $220

(2)(b) Capital, November 30, 199–, $25,523

9–3

a)

Gayle's Reliable Service
Income Statement
For the Month Ended October 31, 199-

Revenue:		
Service Income		1875 50
Expenses:		
Advertising Expense	200 00	
Auto Expense	400 00	
Miscellaneous Expense	50 00	
Telephone Expense	75 00	
Total Expenses		725 00
Net Income		1150 50

b)

Gayle's Reliable Service
Capital Statement
For the Month Ended October 31, 199-

Beginning Balance, Oct. 1, 199-		6302 00
Plus Net Income	1150 50	
Less Withdrawals	600 00	
Net Increase in Capital		550 50
Ending Balance, Oct. 31, 199-		6852 50

c)

Gayle's Reliable Service
Balance Sheet
October 31, 199-

Assets		Liabilities	
Cash	760 00	County Bank & Trust Co.	3600 00
Accounts Receivable	142 50	Owner's Equity	
Automobile	9200 00	Rebecca Gayle, Cap.	6852 50
Supplies	350 00	Total Liab. &	
Total Assets	10452 50	Owner's Equity	10452 50

Chapter 10

10–1 Net Income, $3,350 from completed Income Statement columns on work sheet

		Closing Entries		
199- Dec.	31	Consulting Fees Income	3750 00	
		Royalty Income	500 00	
		Revenue and Expense Summary		4250 00
	31	Revenue and Expense Summary	900 00	
		Advertising Expense		100 00
		Miscellaneous Expense		60 00
		Rent Expense		250 00
		Salary Expense		400 00
		Telephone Expense		90 00
	31	Revenue and Expense Summary	3350 00	
		Gwen Vreeland, Capital		3350 00
	31	Gwen Vreeland, Capital	1800 00	
		Gwen Vreeland, Drawing		1800 00

10–2 Trial Balance amounts:

	Debit		Credit
	800.00		6000.00
	3895.00		12920.00
	4000.00		6500.00
	12500.00	Total	25420.00
	750.00		
	1500.00		
	600.00		
	175.00		
	300.00		
	900.00		
Total	25420.00		

Net Income, $4525.00

10–3 (1) Trial Balance totals, $35,675.75
Net Income, $4,850.00 (on completed work sheet)

10–3 (2)(b)

Carl Alpert
Capital Statement
June 30, 199–

Beginning Balance, April 1		23300 75
Plus: Additional Investment	1000 00	
Net Income	4850 00	
	5850 00	
Less: Withdrawals	4800 00	
Net Increase in Capital		1050 00
Ending Balance, June 30, 199–		24350 75

10–4 (1) net income $1,485.00
(2)(b) Washington, Capital Dec. 31, $7,315.00

Chapter 11

11–1

CASH	DOLLARS	CENTS
CHECKS LIST SINGLY	1049	00
	8	72
	148	65
	79	15
TOTAL ITEMS / TOTAL	1285	52

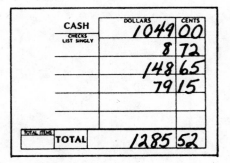

11–2 Balance carried forward on stub No. 120, $106.50
11–3 Correct available balance, $416.90
11–4 Correct available balance, $705.32

Chapter 12

12–1 (3) Replenishing check drawn for $32.25
12–2

Date		Account		Debit	Credit
199- Apr.	1	Petty Cash		35 00	
		Cash			35 00
		To establish fund			
	30	Auto Expense		10 00	
		Delivery Expense		2 75	
		Miscellaneous Expense		7 50	
		Office Expense		12 00	
		Cash			32 25
		To replenish fund			

Cycle One Examination

Part I

1.	T	11.	T
2.	F	12.	T
3.	T	13.	F
4.	T	14.	T
5.	F	15.	F
6.	T	16.	T
7.	T	17.	T
8.	F	18.	F
9.	F	19.	F
10.	F	20.	T

Part II

1.	I	9.	V
2.	L	10.	E
3.	Q	11.	B
4.	U	12.	N
5.	F	13.	A
6.	G	14.	K
7.	R	15.	H
8.	T		

Part III	Account Dr.	Account Cr.
1.	J	A
2.	B	A
3.	A	D
4.	G	F
5.	B	A, C
6.	E	A
7.	F	H, I, J
8.	F	D
9.	D	F
10.	D	E

Part IV (1) Complete Chet Gorski's work sheet.

County-Wide Plumbing
Work Sheet
For the Year Ended December 31, 199-

Account Title	A. N.	Trial Balance Debit	Trial Balance Credit	Income Statement Debit	Income Statement Credit	Balance Sheet Debit	Balance Sheet Credit
Cash	111	1472 50				1472 50	
Petty Cash	112	25 00				25 00	
Accounts Receivable	113	385 00				385 00	
Supplies	114	242 50				242 50	
Truck	115	14850 00				14850 00	
Accounts Payable	211		970 00				970 00
Chet Gorski, Capital	311		14685 00				14685 00
Chet Gorski, Drawing	312	9500 00				9500 00	
Fees Income	411		18620 00		18620 00		
Advertising Expense	511	480 00		480 00			
Automobile Expense	512	2400 00		2400 00			
Miscellaneous Expense	513	120 00		120 00			
Rent Expense	514	3600 00		3600 00			
Telephone Expense	515	1200 00		1200 00			
		34275 00	34275 00	7800 00	18620 00	26475 00	15655 00
Net Income				10820 00			10820 00
				18620 00	18620 00	26475 00	26475 00

Part IV (2)

County-Wide Plumbing
Capital Statement
December 31, 199–

Beginning Capital, Jan. 1, 199–		9685 00
Plus: Additional Investment	5000 00	
Net Income	10820 00	
	15820 00	
Less: Withdrawals	9500 00	
Net Increase in Capital		6320 00
Ending Capital, Dec. 31, 199–		16005 00

Part IV (3)

County-Wide Plumbing
Balance Sheet
December 31, 199–

Assets		Liabilities	
Cash	1472 50	Accounts Payable	970 00
Petty Cash	25 00	Owners' Equity	
Accounts Receivable	385 00	Chet Gorski, Capital	16005 00
Supplies	242 50		
Truck	14850 00	Total Liabilities +	
Total Assets	16975 00	Owners' Equity	16975 00

Part IV (4)

GENERAL JOURNAL

Date		Account	Debit	Credit
		Closing Entries		
199- Dec.	31	Fees Income	18620 00	
		Revenue and Expense Summary		18620 00
	31	Revenue and Expense Summary	7800 00	
		Advertising Expense		480 00
		Automobile Expense		2400 00
		Miscellaneous Expense		120 00
		Rent Expense		3600 00
		Telephone Expense		1200 00
	31	Revenue and Expense Summary	10820 00	
		Chet Gorski, Capital		10820 00
	31	Chet Gorski, Capital	9500 00	
		Chet Gorski, Drawing		9500 00

Part V (1)

NO. 207	$ 35.50	
DATE January 7 19 9-		
TO Wilson Supply Co.		
FOR Smoke alarm (Equipment)		
	DOLLARS	CENTS
BAL. BRO'T FOR'D	382	47
AMT. DEPOSITED	225	00
TOTAL	607	47
AMT. THIS CHECK	35	50
BAL. CAR'D FOR'D	571	97

No. 207

1-830
860

January 7 19 9-

Pay to the order of Wilson Supply Company $35 50/100

Thirty-five & 50/100 Dollars

BOLTON NATIONAL BANK
of New York, NY

Student's Name

⑆0860⑆0830⑆ 1248⑈671⑈

Part V (2)

JOURNAL

199– Jan.	7	Equipment		35 50	
		Cash			35 50
		Bought smoke alarm			

Chapter 13

13–1 (1) and (3)

PURCHASES JOURNAL — Page 5

Date		From Whom Purchased Account Credited	Invoice No.	PR	Purchases Dr. Acct. Pay. Cr.
199– Feb.	3	Dye + Akins	1705	✓	300 00
	10	Edward Kalpakian + Sons	G-116	✓	425 00
	17	Dye + Akins	1751	✓	385 00
	25	Edward Kalpakian + Sons	G-151	✓	500 00
	28	Total			1,610 00
					(51) (21)

13–1 (2)

ACCOUNTS PAYABLE LEDGER

Dye & Akins
1011 Mountain Avenue, Denver, CO 80201

Date			PR	Dr.	Cr.	Cr. Bal.
199- Jan	15		P1		450 00	450 00
Feb.	3		P5		300 00	750 00
	17		P5		385 00	1135 00

Edward Kalpakian & Sons
379 Valley View Drive, Denver, CO 80204

Date			PR	Dr.	Cr.	Cr. Bal.
199- Feb.	10		P5		425 00	425 00
	25		P5		500 00	925 00

13–1 (3)

GENERAL LEDGER

Accounts Payable — No. 21

Date			PR	Dr.	Cr.	Balance Dr.	Balance Cr.
Jan	31		P1		450 00		450 00
199- Feb.	28		P5		1610 00		2010 00

Purchases — No. 51

Date			PR	Dr.	Cr.	Balance Dr.	Balance Cr.
199- Feb.	28		P5	1610 00		1610 00	

13–1 (4)

Ruth Ann Davis
Schedule of Accounts Payable
February 28, 199–

Dye + Akins	1 135 00
Edward Kalpakian + Sons	925 00
Total Accounts Payable	2 060 00

13–2 (4)

Paul Zagretti
Schedule of Accounts Payable
February 28, 199–

Glen Mfg., Inc.	620 00
Island Supply	565 00
Paul Olins	535 00
Gregory Sims	250 00
Wilson + Shea	600 00
Total Accounts Payable	2 570 00

Chapter 14

14–1 (1) and (2)

CASH DISBURSEMENTS JOURNAL Page 3

Date		Account Debited	Ck. No.	PR	General Dr.	Acct. Pay. Dr.	S. Krasnoff Draw. Dr.	Cash Cr.
199- Mar.	1	Rent Expense	247		400 00			400 00
	3	Utilities Expense	248		76 50			76 50
	8	Paula Cory	249			50 00		50 00
	10	Sid Krasnoff, Drawing	250	✓			500 00	500 00
	17	Salary Expense	251		300 00			300 00
	22	Hilda Piper	252			90 00		90 00
	24	Sid Krasnoff, Drawing	253	✓			500 00	500 00
	29	Equipment	254		1 250 00			1 250 00
	31	Salary Expense	255		300 00			300 00
	31	Totals			2 326 50	140 00	1 000 00	3 466 50
					(✓)	( )	( )	( )

14–2 (1), (2), and (4)

PURCHASES JOURNAL Page 2

Date		Account Credited	Invoice No.	PR	Purchases Dr. Acct. Pay. Cr.
199- Apr.	4	Abel Jenks	P-311	✓	600 00
	20	W. T. Gross	S-113	✓	1 450 00
	30	Total			2 050 00
					(51) (21)

14–2 (1), (3), and (4)

CASH DISBURSEMENTS JOURNAL Page 3

Date		Acct. Dr.	Ck. No.	PR	General Dr.	Acct. Pay. Dr.	Cash Cr.
199- Apr.	1	Rent Expense	502	65	450 00		450 00
	8	Helen Scordas, Drawing	503	32	400 00		400 00
	14	Abel & Jenks	504	✓		800 00	800 00
	15	Salary Expense	505	67	325 00		325 00
	22	Supplies	506	15	75 00		75 00
	28	Helen Scordas, Drawing	507	32	500 00		500 00
	30	W. F. Gross	508	✓		725 00	725 00
	30	Totals			1750 00	1525 00	3275 00
					(✓)	(21)	( )

14–2 (2) and (3)

ACCOUNTS PAYABLE LEDGER

Abel & Jenks
140 Rocky Mountain Street, Boise, ID 83701

Date			PR	Dr.	Cr.	Cr. Bal.
199- Apr.	1	Balance	✓			800 00
	4		P2		600 00	1400 00
	14		CD3	800 00		600 00

W. F. Gross
205 Columbia Avenue, Boise, ID 83702

Date			PR	Dr.	Cr.	Cr. Bal.
199- Apr.	20		P2		1450 00	1450 00
	30		CD3	725 00		725 00

GENERAL LEDGER

Cash No. 11

Date			PR	Dr.	Cr.	Balance Dr.	Balance Cr.
199- Apr.	1	Balance	✓			4500 00	
	30		CD3		3275 00	1225 00	

(continued)

14–2 (2) and (3)

Supplies — No. 15

Date			PR	Dr.	Cr.	Balance Dr.	Balance Cr.
199- Apr.	1	Balance	✓			50.00	
	22		CD3	75.00		125.00	

Accounts Payable — No. 21

Date			PR	Dr.	Cr.	Balance Dr.	Balance Cr.
199- Apr.	1	Balance	✓				800.00
	30		P2		2,050.00		2,850.00
	30		CD3	1,525.00			1,325.00

Helen Scordas, Drawing — No. 32

Date			PR	Dr.	Cr.	Balance Dr.	Balance Cr.
199- Apr.	8		CD3	400.00		400.00	
	28		CD3	500.00		900.00	

Purchases — No. 51

Date			PR	Dr.	Cr.	Balance Dr.	Balance Cr.
199- Apr.	30		P2	2,050.00		2,050.00	

Rent Expense — No. 65

Date			PR	Dr.	Cr.	Balance Dr.	Balance Cr.
199- Apr.	1		CD3	450.00		450.00	

Salary Expense — No. 67

Date			PR	Dr.	Cr.	Balance Dr.	Balance Cr.
199- Apr.	15		CD3	325.00		325.00	

14–2 (5)

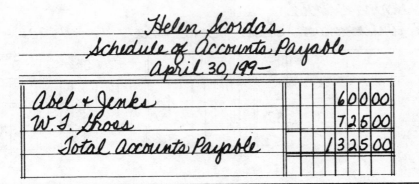

Helen Scordas
Schedule of Accounts Payable
April 30, 199–

Abel & Jenks	600 00
W. T. Gross	725 00
Total Accounts Payable	1325 00

Chapter 15

15–1 (1), (2), and (3)

SALES JOURNAL Page 31

Date		To Whom Sold - Account Debited	Invoice No.	PR	Acct. Rec. Dr. Sales Cr.
199– Mar.	2	Mrs. Edward Ardyce	215	✓	175 00
	9	Mr. Herman Gold	216	✓	96 50
	16	Ms. Eliza Fisher	217	✓	107 30
	23	Mrs. Edward Ardyce	218	✓	62 45
	30	Ms. Eliza Fisher	219	✓	29 50
	31	Total			470 75
					(13) (41)

15–1 (2)

ACCOUNTS RECEIVABLE LEDGER

Mrs. Edward Ardyce
305 Riverview Terrace, Cincinnati, OH 45204

Date				Dr.	Cr.	Dr. Bal.
199– Mar.	2		S31	175 00		175 00
	23		S31	62 45		237 45

Ms. Eliza Fisher
851 Clarkfield Street, Cincinnati, OH 45201

Date				Dr.	Cr.	Dr. Bal.
199– Mar.	16		S31	107 30		107 30
	30		S31	29 50		136 80

(continued)

15–1 (2)

Mr. Herman Gold
79 Willowbrook Drive, Cincinnati, OH 45202

Date				Dr.	Cr.	Dr. Bal.
199– Mar.	1	Balance	✓			258 60
	9		S31	96 50		355 10

GENERAL LEDGER

15–1 (3)

Accounts Receivable — No. 13

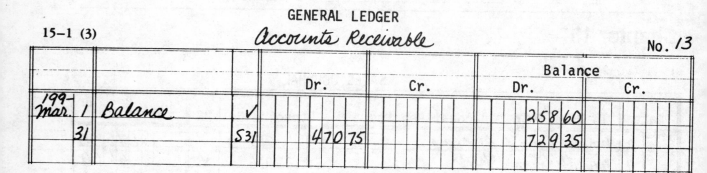

Date				Dr.	Cr.	Balance Dr.	Balance Cr.
199– Mar.	1	Balance	✓			258 60	
	31		S31	470 75		729 35	

Sales — No. 41

Date				Dr.	Cr.	Balance Dr.	Balance Cr.
199– Mar.	31		S31		470 75		470 75

15–1 (4)

Mears Department Store
Schedule of Accounts Receivable
March 31, 199–

Mrs. Edward Ardyce	237 45
Ms. Eliza Fisher	136 80
Mr. Herman Gold	355 10
Total Accounts Receivable	729 35

15–2 (1) and (3)

SALES JOURNAL — Page 8

Date		To Whom Sold - Account Debited	Invoice No.	PR	Acct. Rec. Dr. Sales Cr.
199- Apr.	2	Mrs. Fay Wilamowski	328	✓	47 50
	6	Ms. Shirley Callahan	329	✓	36 95
	9	Mr. William Witt	330	✓	49 25
	13	Shirley Callahan	331	✓	107 65
	16	Mrs. Marjorie Intrator	332	✓	76 80
	20	Fay Wilamowski	333	✓	52 90
	23	William Witt	334	✓	59 20
	27	Marjorie Intrator	335	✓	67 75
	30	Shirley Callahan	336	✓	87 00
	30	Total			585 00
					(13)(41)

15–2 (4)

Winslow's Emporium
Schedule of Accounts Receivable
April 30, 199-

Ms. Shirley Callahan	276 60
Mrs. Marjorie Intrator	144 55
Mrs. Fay Wilamowski	165 70
Mr. William Witt	203 45
Total Accounts Receivable	790 30

Chapter 16

16–1 (1), (2), and (3)

CASH RECEIPTS JOURNAL

Page 6

Date		Account Credited	PR	General Cr.	Accts. Rec. Cr.	Sales Cr.	Cash Dr.
199- Apr.	23		✓	750 00	1435 00	5976 00	8161 00
	23	Raul Garcia, Capital		2000 00			2000 00
	24	Lone Star Bank		2500 00			2500 00
	25	J. R. Dallas			85 00		85 00
	26	Margo Chase			60 00		60 00
	27	Equipment		95 00			95 00
	28	Frances Lima			75 00		75 00
	29	Sales	✓			1765 00	1765 00
	30	Totals		5345 00	1655 00	7741 00	14741 00
				(✓)	(13)	(41)	(11)

(Note: In a complete problem, items listed in the General Cr. and Accts. Rec. Cr. columns would be posted. Post references would appear, therefore, in the PR column.)

16–1 (3)

GENERAL LEDGER

Cash No. 11

Date			PR	Dr.	Cr.	Balance Dr.	Balance Cr.
199- Apr.	1	Balance	✓			1935 00	
	30		CR6	14741 00		16676 00	

Accounts Receivable No. 13

Date			PR	Dr.	Cr.	Balance Dr.	Balance Cr.
199- Apr.	1	Balance	✓			1729 50	
	30		CR6		1655 00	74 50	

Sales No. 41

Date			PR	Dr.	Cr.	Balance Dr.	Balance Cr.
199- Mar.	31		S4		3500 00		3500 00
	31		CR5		6250 00		9750 00
	31		J3	9750 00			—
Apr.	30		CR6		7741 00		7741 00

16–2 (1) and (2)

SALES JOURNAL Page 9

Date		To Whom Sold - Account Debited	Invoice No.	PR	Acct. Rec. Dr. Sales Cr.
199- May	1	Willow's Beauty Shoppe	7156	✓	465 00
	1	Lee's Unisex	7157	✓	395 00
	12	Goddess of Love	7158	✓	268 00
	12	Jayne's Curls + Waves	7159	✓	175 00
	17	Willow's Beauty Shoppe	7160	✓	192 00
	29	Jayne's Curls + Waves	7161	✓	225 00
	29	Lee's Unisex	7162	✓	315 20
	31	Total			2035 20
					(13) (41)

16–2 (1), (2), and (3)

CASH RECEIPTS JOURNAL Page 6

Date		Account Credited	PR	General Cr.	Accts. Rec. Cr.	Sales Cr.	Cash Dr.
199- May	7	Sales	✓			252.50	252.50
	10	Goddess of Love	✓		200.00		200.00
	14	Sales	✓			307.25	307.25
	15	Pat Norrell, Capital	31	3000.00			3000.00
	19	Lee's Unisex	✓		395.00		395.00
	21	Sales	✓			296.80	296.80
	25	Willow's Beauty Shoppe	✓		265.00		265.00
	28	Sales	✓			319.90	319.90
	31	Sales	✓			191.40	191.40
	31	Totals		3000.00	860.00	1367.85	5227.85
				(✓)	(13)	(41)	(11)

GENERAL LEDGER

Cash No. 11

Date			PR	Dr.	Cr.	Balance Dr.	Balance Cr.
199- May	1	Balance	✓			1078.50	
	31		CR6	5227.85		6306.35	

Accounts Receivable No. 13

Date			PR	Dr.	Cr.	Balance Dr.	Balance Cr.
199- May	1	Balance	✓			200.00	
	31		S9	2035.70		2235.70	
			CR6		860.00	1375.70	

Pat Norrell, Capital No. 31

Date			PR	Dr.	Cr.	Balance Dr.	Balance Cr.
199- May	1	Balance	✓				25000.00
	15		CR6		3000.00		28000.00

Sales No. 41

Date			PR	Dr.	Cr.	Balance Dr.	Balance Cr.
199- May	31		S9		2035.70		2035.70
	31		CR6		1367.85		3403.55

16–2 (2) and (3)

ACCOUNTS RECEIVABLE LEDGER

Goddess of Love
110 Chemung Avenue, Binghamton, NY 13901

Date			PR	Dr.	Cr.	Dr. Bal.
199- May	1	Balance	✓			200 00
	10		CR6		200 00	—
	12		S9	268 50		268 50

Jayne's Curls & Waves
39 Tompkins Avenue, Cortland, NY 13045

Date			PR	Dr.	Cr.	Dr. Bal.
199- May	12		S9	175 00		175 00
	29		S9	225 00		400 00

Lee's Unisex
451 College Heights Road, Ithaca, NY 14850

Date			PR	Dr.	Cr.	Dr. Bal.
199- May	1		S9	395 00		395 00
	19		CR6		395 00	—
	29		S9	315 20		315 20

Willow's Beauty Shoppe
58 Swain Boulevard, Elmira, NY 14901

Date			PR	Dr.	Cr.	Dr. Bal.
199- May	1		S9	465 00		465 00
	17		S9	192 00		657 00
	25		CR6		265 00	392 00

16–2 (4)

Pat Norrell
Schedule of Accounts Receivable
May 31, 199–

Goddess of Love	268 50
Jayne's Curls & Waves	400 00
Lee's Unisex	315 20
Willow's Beauty Shoppe	392 00
Total Accounts Receivable	1,375 70

Chapter 17

17–1 (1) and (2)

GENERAL JOURNAL — Page 7

Accts. Pay. Dr.	General Dr.	Date		PR	General Cr.	Accts. Rec. Cr.
	35 00	199– May 2	Sales Returns & Allowances			
			Jane McDonald			35 00
			Credit Memo No. 18			
	65 00	5	Hedy Nachtigal			
			Netty Nachtigal		65 00	
			Correct posting error			
100 00		9	Baldwin Piano Company			
			Purchases Returns & Allowances		100 00	
			Debit Memo No. 53			
	95 00	15	Philip Scheiber, Drawing			
			Purchases		95 00	
			Withdrew guitar for nephew			
	80 00	22	Sales Returns & Allowances			
			Alice Glaser			80 00
			Credit Memo No. 19			
	185 00	29	Equipment			
			Philip Scheiber, Capital		185 00	
			Invested desk			
100 00	460 00	31	Totals		445 00	115 00
	(✓)				(✓)	

17–3

STATEMENT OF ACCOUNT

Hudson's Department Store
100 Gateway Plaza
St. Louis, MO 63101

SOLD TO

Ms. Pearl Nathanson
972 Riverside Dr.
St. Louis, MO 63104

May 20 19 9–

		CHARGES		
May	1		60 00	
	5		75 00	
	18		45 00	
				180 00
		PAYMENTS/CREDITS		
	12		35 00	
	15		20 00	
				55 00
	18	Balance Due		125 00

17–4 (1) and (2)

PURCHASES JOURNAL Page 10

Date		Account Credited			PR	Purchases Dr. Acct. Pay. Cr.
199- May	17	Schmidt & Brendle				375.00
	17	Winston Jewelers				1,200.00
	31	Totals				1,575.00
						( ) ( )

17–4 (1) and (2)

SALES JOURNAL Page 14

Date		Account Debited	Invoice No.	PR	Accts. Rec. Dr. Sales Cr.
199- May	4	Antonio Lorenzo	B192		300.00
	4	Edward Grabezak	B193		250.00
	11	Marc Green	B194		275.00
	31	Totals			825.00
					( ) ( )

17–4 (1)

CASH RECEIPTS JOURNAL Page 19

Date				PR	Gen. Cr.	Acct. Rec. Cr.	Sales Cr.	Cash Dr.
199- May	1	Balance on hand	$1,500	✓				
	3	Marc Green				150.00		150.00
	3	Gian Polidoro				95.00		95.00
	22	Antonio Lorenzo				50.00		50.00
	23	Edward Grabezak				125.00		125.00
	31	Sales		✓			2,740.00	2,740.00
	31	Totals			—	420.00	2,740.00	3,160.00
					(✓)	( )	( )	( )

17–4 (1)

CASH DISBURSEMENTS JOURNAL

Date			Ck. No.	PR	Gen. Dr.	Accts. Pay Dr.	Purch. Dr.	Cash Cr.
199- May	1	Winslow Jewelers	392			46500		46500
	1	Rent Expense	393		45000			45000
	13	Edward Shaw, Drawing	394		50000			50000
	14	Salary Expense	395		30000			30000
	28	Schmidt & Brendle	396			37500		37500
	29	Sales Returns & Allowances	397		4000			4000
	31	Totals			129000	84000	—	213000
					(✓)	( )		( )

17–4 (1)

GENERAL JOURNAL

Page 5

Acct. Pay. Dr.	Gen. Dr.	Date			PR	Gen. Cr.	Acct. Rec. Cr.
	3500	199- May	8	Supplies			
				Equipment		3500	
				Posting Error			
	7500		24	Sales Returns & Allowances			
				Marc Green			7500
				Credit Memo No. 35			
	20000		31	Edward Shaw, Drawing			
				Purchases		20000	
				Ring for wife			
—	31000		31	Totals		23500	7500
(–)	(✓)					(✓)	( )

Chapter 18

18–1

Daniel Green
Work Sheet
For Quarter Year Ended June 30, 19—

Account Title	A. N.	Trial Balance Debit	Trial Balance Credit	Adjustments Debit	Adjustments Credit	Income Statement Debit	Income Statement Credit	Balance Sheet Debit	Balance Sheet Credit
Cash		1200.00						1200.00	
Accounts Receivable		2500.00						2500.00	
Merchandise Inventory		5000.00		(B) 5175.00	(A) 5000.00			5175.00	
Equipment		6000.00						6000.00	
Supplies		400.00			(C) 100.00			300.00	
Accounts Payable			1800.00						1800.00
Daniel Green, Capital			14200.00						14200.00
Daniel Green, Drawing		1500.00						1500.00	
Revenue and Expense Summary				(A) 5000.00	(B) 5175.00	5000.00	5175.00		
Sales			6500.00				6500.00		
Sales Returns & Allowances		250.00				250.00			
Purchases		3000.00				3000.00			
Purchases Returns & Allowances			150.00				150.00		
Miscellaneous Expense		100.00				100.00			
Rent Expense		1200.00				1200.00			
Salary Expense		1500.00				1500.00			
Supplies Expense				(C) 100.00		100.00			
		22650.00	22650.00	10275.00	10275.00	11150.00	11825.00	16675.00	16000.00
Net Income						675.00			675.00
						11825.00	11825.00	16675.00	16675.00

18–2

Timothy Sullivan
Work Sheet
For Month Ended January 31, 199-

Account Title	A. N.	Trial Balance Debit	Trial Balance Credit	Adjustments Debit	Adjustments Credit	Income Statement Debit	Income Statement Credit	Balance Sheet Debit	Balance Sheet Credit
Cash		336000						336000	
Accounts Receivable		351500						351500	
Merchandise Inventory		380000		(B) 395000	(A) 380000			395000	
Supplies		32500			(C) 12000			20500	
Prepaid Insurance		30000			(D) 5000			25000	
Accounts Payable			180000						180000
Timothy Sullivan, Capital			787500						787500
Timothy Sullivan, Drawing		300000						30000	
Revenue and Expense Summary				(A) 380000	(B) 395000	380000	395000		
Sales			420000				420000		
Sales Returns + Allowances		3500				3500			
Purchases		170000				170000			
Advertising Expense		10000				10000			
Insurance Expense				(D) 5000		5000			
Miscellaneous Expense		4000				4000			
Rent Expense		40000				40000			
Supplies Expense				(C) 12000		12000			
		1387500	1387500	792000	792000	624500	815000	1158000	967500
Net Income						190500			190500
						815000	815000	1158000	1158000

Chapter 19

19–1 (1)

Daniel Green
Income Statement
For Quarter Ended April 30, 199–

Income:			
Sales		650000	
Less Sales Returns and Allowances		25000	
Net Sales			625000
Cost of Goods Sold:			
Merchandise Inventory, Apr. 1		500000	
Purchases	3000		
Less Purchases Ret. + Allow	150		
Net Purchases		285000	
Merchandise Available for Sale		785000	
Less Merchandise Inv., June 30		517500	
Cost of Goods Sold			267500
Gross Profit on Sales			357500
Expenses:			
Miscellaneous Expense		10000	
Rent Expense		120000	
Salary Expense		150000	
Supplies Expense		10000	
Total Expense			290000
Net Income			67500

19–1 (2)

Daniel Green
Capital Statement
For Quarter Ended June 30, 199-

Beginning Balance, April 1		12200 00
Plus: Additional Investment	2000 00	
Net Income	675 00	
	2675 00	
Less: Withdrawals	1500 00	
Net Increase in Capital		1175 00
Ending Balance, June 30		13375 00

19–1 (3)

Daniel Green
Balance Sheet
June 30, 199-

Assets		
Cash	1200 00	
Accounts Receivable	2500 00	
Merchandise Inventory	5175 00	
Equipment	6000 00	
Supplies	300 00	
Total Assets		15175 00
Liabilities		
Accounts Payable		1800 00
Owner's Equity		13375 00
Total Liabilities and Owner's Equity		15175 00

19–2 (2)

Timothy Sullivan
Capital Statement
For Month Ended January 31, 199–

Beginning Balance, Jan. 1		5375 00
Additional Investment		2500 00
		7875 00
Plus: Net Income	1905 00	
Less Withdrawals	300 00	
Net Increase in Capital		1605 00
Ending Balance, Jan. 31		9480 00

or

Timothy Sullivan
Capital Statement
For Month Ended January 31, 199–

Beginning Balance, Jan. 1		5375 00
Plus: Additional Investment	2500 00	
Net Income	1905 00	
	4405 00	
Less: Withdrawals	300 00	
Net Increase in Cap.		4105 00
Ending Balance, Jan. 31		9480 00

19–2 (3) Assets $11,280 = Liabilities $1,800 + Owner's Equity $9,480.

19–3 (1)

Abdullah and Pahlevi
Work Sheet
For Year Ended December 31, 19—

Account Title	A. N.	Trial Balance Debit	Trial Balance Credit	Adjustments Debit	Adjustments Credit	Income Statement Debit	Income Statement Credit	Balance Sheet Debit	Balance Sheet Credit
Cash		3625 00						3625 00	
Accounts Receivable		18260 00						18260 00	
Merchandise Inventory, Jan. 1		22320 00		(B) 23195 00	(A) 22320 00			23195 00	
Equipment		7500 00						7500 00	
Prepaid Insurance		500 00			(C) 100 00			400 00	
Supplies		275 00			(D) 96 50			178 50	
Accounts Payable			3105 00						3105 00
I. G. Abdullah, Capital			33802 00						33802 00
I. G. Abdullah, Drawing		10000 00						10000 00	
S. H. Pahlevi, Capital			28404 00						28404 00
S. H. Pahlevi, Drawing		12000 00						12000 00	
Revenue and Expense Summary				(A) 22320 00	(B) 23195 00	22320 00	23195 00		
Sales			51790 00				51790 00		
Sales Returns and Allowances		2570 00				2570 00			
Purchases		31380 00				31380 00			
Purchases Returns and Allowances			1529 00				1529 00		
Advertising Expense		600 00				600 00			
Insurance Expense				(C) 100 00		100 00			
Rent Expense		3600 00				3600 00			
Salary Expense		6000 00				6000 00			
Supplies Expense				(D) 96 50		96 50			
		118630 00	118630 00	45711 50	45711 50	66666 50	76514 00	75158 50	65311 00
Net Income						9847 50			9847 50
						76514 00	76514 00	75158 50	75158 50

19–3 (3)	T. G. Abdullah	
	Ending Balance, Dec. 31	29,429.14
	S. H. Pahlevi	
	Ending Balance, Dec. 31	20,624.36
	Total Owners' Equity	50,053.50

Chapter 20

20–1 (1) and (2)

GENERAL JOURNAL — Page 7

Debit	Date		Description	Credit
			Adjusting Entries	
5000 00	199- June	30	Revenue and Expense Summary	
			Merchandise Inventory	5000 00
5175 00		30	Merchandise Inventory	
			Revenue and Expense Summary	5175 00
100 00		30	Supplies Expense	
			Supplies	100 00
			Closing Entries	
6500 00		30	Sales	
150 00			Purchases Returns and Allowances	
			Revenue and Expense Summary	6650 00
6150 00		30	Revenue and Expense Summary	
			Sales Returns and Allowances	250 00
			Purchases	3000 00
			Miscellaneous Expense	100 00
			Rent Expense	1200 00
			Salary Expense	1500 00
			Supplies Expense	100 00
675 00		30	Revenue and Expense Summary	
			Daniel Green, Capital	675 00
1500 00		30	Daniel Green, Capital	
			Daniel Green, Drawing	1500 00

20–2 (3)

Timothy Sullivan
Post-closing Trial Balance
January 31, 199–

Account	Debit	Credit
Cash	3360.00	
Accounts Receivable	3515.00	
Merchandise Inventory	3950.00	
Supplies	205.00	
Prepaid Insurance	250.00	
Accounts Payable		1800.00
Timothy Sullivan, Capital		9480.00
Totals	11280.00	11280.00

20–3 (3)

Abdullah and Pahlevi
Post-closing Trial Balance
December 31, 199–

Account	Debit	Credit
Cash	3625.00	
Accounts Receivable	18260.00	
Merchandise Inventory	23195.00	
Equipment	7500.00	
Prepaid Insurance	400.00	
Supplies	178.50	
Accounts Payable		3105.00
T. G. Abdullah, Capital		29429.14
S. H. Pahlevi, Capital		20624.36
Totals	53158.50	53158.50

Chapter 21

21–1 (1), (2), and (3)

COMBINATION JOURNAL p. 5

General Dr.	General Cr.	Date	Explanation	PR	Cash Dr.	Cash Cr.	House. Exp. Dr.	Auto Exp. Dr.
		199- May 1	Balance $1,675—	✓				
		1	Rent	✓		695 00	695 00	
37 95		3	Personal Expenses			37 95		
		5	Gas for Car	✓		14 60		14 60
		8	Electric Bill	✓		79 50	79 50	
63 45		10	Food Shopping			63 45		
		12	Household Ins.	✓		108 75	108 75	
	1048 30	15	Salary Income		1048 30			
		21	Automobile Ins.	✓		355 20		355 20
59 25		24	Food Shopping			59 25		
48 95		25	Personal Expenses			48 95		
		26	Auto tune-up	✓		66 50		66 50
80 00		28	Medical Bill			80 00		
	1048 30	29	Salary Income		1048 30			
91 85		30	Charge Accts.			91 85		
		31	Telephone Bill	✓		54 30	54 30	
381 45	2096 60	31	Totals		2096 60	1755 30	937 55	436 30

	General Dr.	General Cr.
21-2 (2)	115.00	2400.00

Cash Dr.	Cash Cr.	Household Dr.	Medical Dr.
2400.00	1531.84	1274.34	142.50

(3) $2,030.16

21–3 (1), (2), and (3)

COMBINATION JOURNAL

General Dr.	General Cr.	Date	Explanation	PR	Cash Dr.	Cash Cr.	Accounts Receivable Dr.	Accounts Receivable Cr.	Fee Income Cr.	Accounts Payable Dr.	Accounts Payable Cr.	Office Exp. Dr.	Travel & Auto Exp. Dr.
		19– June 1	Cash Balance 1042.35	✓									
650 00		1	Rent Expense			650 00							
		3	Stationery & Cards			32 90						32 90	
		5	H.L. Thompson				4362 40		4362 40				
2250 00		8	Furn. & Fixture			750 00					1500 00		
		11	Telephone			67 88						67 88	
		15	Legal Forms			28 25						28 25	
		20	Tolls & Mileage			16 50							16 50
		22	Rec'd. Thompson		4362 40			4362 40					
350 00		24	File Cabinet			350 00							
		27	Postage			10 00						10 00	
		29	Gasoline			14 00							14 00
1200 00		30	Paula Davis Draw.			1200 00							
	350 00	30	File Cabinet		350 00								
4450 00	350 00	30	Totals		4712 40	3119 53	4362 40	4362 40	4362 40	—	1500 00	139 03	30 50
(✓)	(✓)				( )	( )	( )	( ) *	—	—	( )	( )	( )
			(3) Balance, June 1		$1042 35								
			Cash Dr.		+ 4712 40								
					5754 75								
			Cash Cr.		−3119 53								
			Balance, June 30		$2635 22								

* For tax purposes, $362.40 would be separated from Income, inasmuch as they are reimbursed expenses. A separate record should be kept for this item, or set it up as another special column in this journal.

21–4 (1), (2), (3) and (4)

COMBINATION JOURNAL

Cash Dr.	Cash Cr.	Line	Date 199_		PR	General Dr.	General Cr.	Accounts Receivable Dr.	Accounts Receivable Cr.	Sales Credit	Accounts Payable Dr.	Accounts Payable Cr.	Purchases Dr.
		1	June 1	Balance $5,162	✓								
	1200 00	2	1	Rent Expense		1200 00							
		3	3	Smythe Co.				1950 00		1950 00			
	1600 00	4	5	Maxwell, Inc.							1600 00		
995 00		5	8	PVP & Co.					995 00				
		6	12	Khan & Farah								3000 00	3000 00
	62 50	7	13	Office Supplies		62 50							
	2000 00	8	15	Salary Expense		2000 00							
1535 50		9	19	Bill Bros.					1535 50				
	125 00	10	21	Advertising Exp.		125 00							
	350 00	11	24	Bayer, Drawing		350 00							
	350 00	12	24	Falk, Drawing		350 00							
		13	27	Beck & Pesky Inc.								1500 00	1500 00
	1000 00	14	29	Khan & Farah							1000 00		
	182 75	15	30	Telephone Exp.		182 75							
1950 00		16	30	Smythe Co.					1950 00				
250 00		17	30	Office Equip.			250 00						
4730 50	6870 25	18	30	Totals		4270 25	250 00	1950 00	4480 50	1950 00	2600 00	4500 00	4500 00
		19				(✓)	(✓)	( )	( )	( )	( )	( )	( )
		20											
		21											
		22											
		23		(4) June 1 Balance		5162 00							
		24		Cash Dr. total		4730 50							
		25				9892 50							
		26		Cash Cr. total		6270 25							
		27		June 30, Balance		3622 25							
		28											
		29											
		30											

Cycle Two Examination

Part I

1.	T	11.	F
2.	T	12.	T
3.	T	13.	F
4.	F	14.	F
5.	F	15.	T
6.	T	16.	F
7.	T	17.	F
8.	F	18.	T
9.	F	19.	T
10.	T	20.	T

Part II

1.	M	6.	F
2.	J	7.	L
3.	N	8.	A
4.	C	9.	B
5.	H	10.	O

Part III (1)

GENERAL JOURNAL Page 3

Accts. Pay. Dr.	General Dr.	Date		PR	General Cr.	Accts. Rec. Cr.
	5000	199– June 8	Jordan Glaser, Drawing			
			Purchases		5000	
			Withdrew Merchandise			
	1500	12	Sales Returns and Allowances			
			Dr. George Tyler			1500
—	6500	30	Totals		5000	1500
—	(✓)				(✓)	( )

Part III (1)

PURCHASES JOURNAL Page 3

Date		Account Credited	PR	Purchases Dr. Accts. Pay. Cr.
199– June	3	J. L. Rossini Company		500 00
	29	Fred Pulaski Wholesalers, Inc.		300 00
	30	Total		800 00
				( ) ( )

Part III (1)

SALES JOURNAL Page 3

Date		Account Debited		PR	Accts. Rec. Dr. Sales Cr.
199- June	5	Dr. George Tyler			165 00
	26	Mel Guberman			125 00
	30	Total			290 00
					( ) ( )

Part III (1)

CASH RECEIPTS JOURNAL Page 4

Date				PR	General Cr.	Accts. Rec. Cr.	Sales Cr.	Cash Dr.
199- June	1	Balance on hand	$2,500	✓				
	15	Sales		✓			2950 00	2950 00
	22	Dr. George Tyler				150 00		150 00
	30	Sales		✓			3750 00	3750 00
	30	Totals			—	150 00	6700 00	6850 00
					(✓)	( )	( )	( )

Part III (1)

CASH DISBURSEMENTS JOURNAL Page 3

Date		Account Debited	Ck. No.	PR	General Dr.	Accts. Pay. Dr.	Purchases Dr.	Salary Exp. Dr.	Cash Cr.
199- June	1	Rent Expense	147		375 00				375 00
	10	J. L. Rossini Company	148			500 00			500 00
	19	Telephone (Utilities) Expense	149		46 00				46 00
	30	Totals			421 00	500 00	—	—	921 00
					(✓)	( )			( )

Part IV (1)

Fowler's Crystal Palace
Income Statement
For Year Ended December 31, 199-

Income:			
Sales		40,590.00	
Less Sales Returns and Allowances		1,875.00	
Net Sales			38,715.00
Cost of Goods Sold:			
Merchandise Inventory, Jan. 1		10,790.00	
Purchases	21,630		
Less Purchases Ret + Allow.	785		
Net Purchases		20,835.00	
Merchandise Available for Sale		31,625.00	
Less Merchandise Inventory, Dec. 31		12,080.00	
Cost of Goods Sold			19,545.00
Gross Profit on Sales			19,170.00
Expenses:			
Advertising Expense		1,200.00	
Insurance Expense		500.00	
Miscellaneous Expense		240.00	
Rent Expense		3,000.00	
Salary Expense		6,000.00	
Supplies Expense		220.00	
Total Expense			11,160.00
Net Income			8,010.00

Part IV (2)

Fowler's Crystal Palace
Capital Statement
For Year Ended December 31, 199–

Beginning Balance, Jan. 1		25525 00
Additional Investment		1000 00
		26525 00
Less: Withdrawals	12000 00	
Less Net Income	8010 00	
Decrease in Capital		3990 00
Ending Balance, Dec. 31		22535 00

Part IV (3)

Fowler's Crystal Palace
Balance Sheet
December 31, 199–

Assets		
Cash	2400 00	
Accounts Receivable	3850 00	
Merchandise Inventory	12080 00	
Furniture and Fixtures	8500 00	
Prepaid Insurance	100 00	
Supplies	105 00	
Total Assets		27035 00
Liabilities		
Accounts Payable		4500 00
Owner's Equity		
Dina Fowler, Capital		22535 00
Total Liabilities and Owner's Equity		27035 00

Part IV (4)

GENERAL JOURNAL

Page

Accts. Pay. Dr.	General Dr.	Date			PR	General Cr.	Accts. Rec. Cr.
		199–		*Adjusting Entries*			
	10790 00	Dec.	31	Revenue and Expense Summary			
				Merchandise Inventory		10790 00	
	12080 00		31	Merchandise Inventory			
				Revenue and Expense Summary		12080 00	
	500 00		31	Insurance Expense			
				Prepaid Insurance		500 00	
	220 00		31	Supplies Expense			
				Supplies		220 00	
				Closing Entries			
	40590 00		31	Sales			
	795 00			Purchases Returns and Allowances			
				Revenue and Expense Summary		41385 00	
	34665 00		31	Revenue and Expense Summary			
				Sales Returns and Allowances		1875 00	
				Purchases		21630 00	
				Advertising Expense		1200 00	
				Insurance Expense		500 00	
				Miscellaneous Expense		240 00	
				Rent Expense		3000 00	
				Salary Expense		6000 00	
				Supplies Expense		220 00	
	8010 00		31	Revenue and Expense Summary			
				Dina Fowler, Capital		8010 00	
	12000 00		31	Dina Fowler, Capital			
				Dina Fowler, Drawing		12000 00	

INDEX

NOTES

NOTES

NOTES

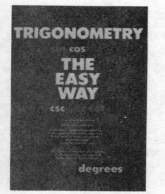

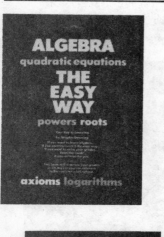